I0798768

What Every Multilingual Student Should Know About Writing for College

Shanti Bruce

Alan S. Kennedy

PEARSON

Boston Columbus Indianapolis New York San Francisco Upper Saddle River
Amsterdam Cape Town Dubai London Madrid Milan Munich Paris Montreal Toronto
Delhi Mexico City Sao Paulo Sydney Hong Kong Seoul Singapore Taipei Tokyo

Executive Editor: Suzanne Phelps-Chambers
Director of Marketing: Megan Galvin
Development Editor: Paul Sarkis
Senior Supplements Editor: Donna Campion
Project Coordination, Text Design, and Electronic Page Makeup: Grapevine Publishing Services, Inc.
Copyeditor: Leslie Ballard
Cover Designer: Alison Barth Burgoyne
Senior Manufacturing Buyer: Roy Pickering
Printer and Binder: R.R. Donnelley Crawfordsville
Cover Printer: R.R. Donnelley Crawfordsville

Please visit us at www.pearsonhighered.com

3 2026

PEARSON

www.pearsonhighered.com

ISBN 10: 0-205-23008-3
ISBN 13: 978-0-205-23008-2

Contents

PREFACE

Learning to use English in an appropriate style for college can be a new endeavor for many students. It can seem like a daunting task, and some have even compared learning academic English to learning a new language. While not a new language altogether, it certainly is a different variety of English. Academic English is what you would expect to read in your textbooks and in scholarly journals, and it is what you will be expected to use in your writing for college courses. It is much more formal than what you would likely use with your friends and family. It follows, then, that becoming comfortable with academic English can be even more challenging for students who regularly speak languages other than English. For these students, many aspects of English itself may be new.

More than ever before, U.S. colleges are finding that the students enrolling in their courses are greatly diverse. They come from a range of places and speak a range of languages. This broader diversity enriches the college experience for everyone. When students bring multiple life experiences and cultural backgrounds to the classroom, class discussions are enhanced and opportunities for learning are multiplied. While this diversity is a welcome addition, it can also pose great challenges. Students from all backgrounds must learn to understand and use academic English in order to communicate effectively with their professors and to understand the information in their chosen disciplines. Likewise, professors must find ways to help all of these different students learn to navigate the world of academic English.

The multiplicity of languages spoken by students is so diverse that it is impossible to assign labels that include everyone. Labels such as *ESL* (English as a second language) or *nonnative speaker* or *international speaker* cover some multilingual students, but they leave out the large group of multilingual students who have grown up here and attended U.S. schools their whole lives. These students, who are native to the United States, may speak languages other than English at home and may not have even begun learning English until elementary school, or even later. Some of these students say they can't determine which language is their first or second, since they often find themselves thinking in two or more languages and mixing languages. They can't label themselves or their language. Because of this, we will avoid common labels as well. The title of this book refers to multilinguals because we wish to acknowledge the main audience for the text, without assumptions about where people come from and how many different languages or dialects of English they might speak.

Therefore, this guide offers tips for all students navigating some of the common pitfalls when learning to understand and use academic English. Language teachers often point out that gaining proficiency in a new language or a new variety of a language, such as academic English, is not just one task; rather, it involves four separate but interrelated skills—all of which require practice, and there is no guarantee that you will make progress with all of them at the same time. These skills are (1) listening, (2) speaking, (3) reading, and (4) writing. Mastering the four skills as they apply to academic English is not an easy endeavor, but with practice, you can do it!

1

WHAT TO EXPECT

Taking a college-level course

Starting college is a new and exciting adventure for all students. Students who come from the United States, as well as from other countries, will find themselves in unfamiliar settings, with professors who have high expectations of them. If you are not used to speaking English regularly, you will have added challenges, but rest assured that everyone in college is facing the same challenge of learning to navigate academic English in this unique academic setting.

Most classes begin by reviewing the course *syllabus*, and this is where you will find contact information for the instructor as well as the course description, course objectives, and required textbooks and materials. The class schedule, assignments, and grading system will also likely be included. If anything on the syllabus is unclear, or you need assistance at any time, ask your professor for help. It may be intimidating at first, but remember that professors want you to succeed. They hold special office hours just so you will have an opportunity to meet with them, and most professors are available by email throughout the week.

In a U.S. college classroom, you will be expected to *participate*. This means that the professor will expect to hear your voice asking questions and sharing opinions. If you come from a family or academic culture where young people are not encouraged to speak up, it is only natural that you might be hesitant to participate. Also, students who are not used to speaking English could be reluctant to jump into conversations with people who seem fluent and confident with the language. Our advice is to push yourself to join the conversations. Participating in class will help you get more out of the lessons, and it will show the professor and the other students that you care about the class and are engaged with the material. Class participation is often a component of a course grade. If you stay too quiet, your final grade can be negatively affected, and even worse, you will miss out on learning all you can, getting to know your classmates, and enjoying the full academic experience.

When you do speak up, remember that it is fine to show that you are unclear about a concept or an assignment. Some students hold back because they think that asking a question makes them look bad in the eyes of the professor or the other students. Actually, it is very likely that if you have a question, another student will have the same question and will benefit from hearing the answer you are given. The professor will appreciate your interest in the class, and the other students will most likely be grateful for the clarification. If you are still working on your English speaking skills, you might make some pronunciation or word-choice errors when you talk in class. This is completely acceptable. Your classmates and your professor will not expect you to speak perfect academic English. The classroom is a place of learning—everyone is welcome and expected to participate, regardless of their level of English proficiency.

Furthermore, in the worlds of academia and research, there is an ever-increasing number of nonnative speakers of English who are using English in their areas of expertise. This means that your professor will likely have colleagues who are working to improve their academic English skills, and it's possible that your professor will be, too.

In addition to asking questions, students in U.S. colleges are expected to have opinions and share them with the class. *Critical thinking* is an important concept in college: This is the process by which you take information or ideas—for example, written material that you read for class—think about the material, and then *form your own point of view* about the material. Very often in college writing assignments, professors will ask you to use critical thinking to analyze some idea, issue, text, or creative work, and then you will be asked to write about it using your opinions. See more about critical thinking in "Critical thinking and academic success" on page 4.

Here are a few key tips to help you succeed in college courses:

1. Don't be afraid to speak up in class by asking questions and expressing your opinions.
2. Be respectful of the opinions of other students. If you disagree with someone, politely make it clear that you disagree with his or her point of view, rather than criticizing or verbally attacking the person.
3. Go to every class, and don't be late. Punctuality is important: it demonstrates your respect for the professor and the course.
4. If you must miss a class, send the instructor an email in which you apologize for the absence and ask what you can do to make sure you do not fall behind in the work.
5. You are fully responsible for getting the details of any assignments that you have missed. It is not the professor's responsibility to contact you about them. If the assignments are not posted online, ask a classmate for his or her email address or phone number so that you can find out about assignments you may have missed.
6. When you write and speak in college, you are expected to use *academic English*. This is a specific variety of English, and it is most likely not the way you usually speak to friends and family in informal settings. Academic English has its own vocabulary, patterns, and aims, which make it different from other kinds of written and spoken English. The more you practice reading and writing academic English, the more comfortable you will be with its special tone and patterns. The suggestions in chapter 2 can help you reach this goal.

Getting help

If you are not sure about how to complete an assignment or have other questions about a course, you should always ask your professor for help. If you bypass your professor and simply guess about something, you are likely to get it wrong, and your learning and grades will suffer. Making an appointment to meet with your professor also demonstrates your dedication to the course.

Many students find that they need clarification when it comes to assignment requirements. Here are some common questions:

1. How long should the writing assignment be?
2. How will the assignment be graded?
3. How do I find appropriate sources for the assignment? (See "Using sources" on page 41.)
4. How do I contact a librarian for help?
5. Are there writing tutors available to help me?
6. Should the writing assignment adhere to a certain citation style?

You may also have general questions for your professor. You might ask:

7. How am I doing in the class in general?
8. Are there areas in which you think I need to improve?

Colleges often have writing centers where students can go for help with written work. Sometimes, these centers are called *learning centers* or *tutoring centers*. Some are called *academic services*, and still others are called *centers for excellence in writing*. Though the names may change, they all have the same goal: to help student writers improve their skills. We recommend you find these helpful places on campus and take advantage of their services.

All students benefit from the help these centers provide, but multilingual students may find them to be even more important to their success in college. Once you locate the center on your campus, find out how and when you can make appointments to meet with a tutor. If you feel you have particular problems with the English language, make them known when you make your appointment. Some tutors might have specific training or more experience working with those particular language issues, so giving them this information in advance will direct you to the person who can be most helpful to you.

Critical thinking and academic success

As we mentioned earlier, critical thinking is a key concept in American education. Academia favors those students who are able to form their own clear point of view about class material by using life experiences and making connections. Critical thinking involves questioning statements, opinions, and assumptions made by others. For example, when you watch a television news broadcast and feel that an issue has not been presented in an even-handed or objective way, you are thinking critically. If a U.S. newspaper article discusses your home country, or a country you have visited and know well, and you don't feel it is accurate, you are thinking critically.

Critical thinking may also refer to the skill of synthesizing information, making inferences, and seeing connections. If a politician describes a policy, and you notice that this policy is a combination of two other policies proposed by two other politicians, this is also a form of critical thinking. When a teacher asks you to compare and contrast the French Revolution with the American Revolution, this requires critical thinking. Following are two examples of questions that do not require critical thinking:

1. What is the boiling point of water?
2. What is the fastest recorded running time of a cheetah?

In contrast, if you were asked to respond to the following situations, you would need to do some critical thinking:

1. Today, many young males choose to wear sagging pants. It is a fashion statement that originated in hip-hop culture and has caught on with people from all races and regions in the United States. Some cities have passed laws banning this fashion choice, and those who continue to wear their pants this way must pay a fine if they are caught. Some people believe this is good because they consider it indecent exposure if underwear is showing. Others, such as the American Civil Liberties Union (ACLU) and the National Association for the Advancement of Colored People (NAACP), oppose restrictions on styles of dress and self-expression and believe these laws are unjust and should be repealed. Do these laws ultimately protect or harm the rights of the American public?
2. Recently, airlines have been kicking passengers off for anything they consider to be unacceptable behavior. A woman was asked to leave because she was crying and requested a

> glass of wine. The flight attendant said she had had too much even though she had not had any. Actually, the woman was afraid of flying and upset about a family illness. A man was removed because he was too tall. At 6′9″, he could not completely remove his legs from the aisle, so he had to leave. Another man had to leave because he was cursing, causing the flight attendant to believe he would be disruptive. Still another man was "deplaned" because of pungent body odor, and two others, a college football player and a rock star, were made to leave because their pants were sagging too low. Finally, a girl was removed because she had a terrible bout of coughing. An in-flight doctor said she was fine, but the airline insisted she leave. Some people believe it is important for airlines to enforce any rule they see fit in order to keep flights safe for everyone. Others believe airlines should not be allowed to kick passengers off unless they are proven, serious threats to the safety of others. Should airlines have the right to decide what is acceptable on their planes?

As you can see, different people will have different ideas about these situations.

Commonly, students will be expected to give their point of view and provide reasons, or support, for their opinions. If you have never been asked to think critically, this may be new territory for you. In some countries' education systems, more emphasis is placed on the skills of memorization, repetition of information, or knowing the right and wrong answers to questions. In certain kinds of U.S. college courses, these skills will not be the focus. Instead, you will be asked to present your opinions, assess and evaluate ideas and texts, and show originality of thought. If this is new to you, it's not a problem. It is an important skill, and you will be able to develop it over time.

2

Academic Skills

Listening

Comprehension challenges

Listening comprehension is very important in a classroom setting. Not only is it important that you understand the lectures and your professor's comments about the subject material and assignments, but you also need to understand your fellow students. For multilingual students, listening skills might be stronger than speaking skills. However, your listening skills may present you with certain challenges. Often, the source of comprehension problems for students is in simply not knowing certain words the speaker uses. Even those who have spoken English their whole lives will be challenged by new words and concepts in the college classroom. The language of certain disciplines could give all students trouble.

Students have accents, but so do some instructors. They may be regional accents. For example, people who grew up in Boston or the Deep South often have recognizable accents. Professors who speak English as a second language may also have accents from their native languages. If you find yourself having trouble understanding your professor, or even your classmates, because of accents, you may have trouble comprehending what you are hearing. If you are speaking one-on-one with a professor or classmate, you can always ask him or her to please slow down or repeat a statement. In a classroom setting, however, it may not always be appropriate to interrupt someone who is speaking to ask for clarification. You may be allowed to record the class on a handheld recording device so that you can play it back later, and you can always follow up with the professor about the content of the discussion during office hours, but you should try to improve your listening skills so that you will be able to follow the class discussions and lectures as they happen. Following are some strategies you can use to increase your comprehension of spoken English:

Phrasal verbs, idioms, and academic language

Phrasal verbs (two- or three-word verbs like *check out* or *make up for*) are very common in English—even in academic English. Phrasal verbs must be memorized just like any other vocabulary. If you know the meaning of *look*, *up*, and *to*, but not the three-word phrasal verb *look up to* (which means "to admire"), you will miss a speaker's meaning. When you study vocabulary, concentrate on learning phrasal verbs. Even in an academic lecture, a speaker may use many phrasal verbs. If he or she uses ones which are not familiar to you, you might miss some of the key ideas. For more on phrasal verbs, see chapter 4, page 79.

Idioms, like phrasal verbs, are *figurative* language. In a phrase like "he threw in the towel," you might know the meaning of all five of those words, but you still might not know the meaning of the idiom. It means "he gave up." If you do not know enough common English idioms, you may find yourself lost when you listen to others speak. Make it part of your vocabulary study to learn idioms. See chapter 4, page 96 for more on idioms.

Academic lectures naturally use academic language. This might be vocabulary specific to the discipline. For example, words like *velocity* and *fulcrum* are used in physics but are not usually used in everyday English. In addition to discipline-specific academic language, there are general academic English words that you should know for general academic success. For example, words like *intrinsic*, *synthesize*, and *penultimate* may be used in a variety of academic disciplines and contexts. The best method for ongoing academic language learning is to read academic-style texts. You can also familiarize yourself with the academic word list. See page 14 for more on this list.

Listening and reading simultaneously

Many books are available as audio books. These are recordings of someone—usually the author or hired voice actors—reading the exact text of a book. They can be purchased or borrowed from a library, and many are also available as audio files to download or stream online. Listening to spoken, academic English while you read the text strengthens your ability to understand what you hear. You can also stop the recording to look up new vocabulary.

In addition to audio books, you should listen to news broadcasts and lectures on television and online. The more familiar you become with academic English, the more comfortable you will be using it in your speaking and writing in college. Two excellent free online resources are listed below. In both cases, you can chose topics that are of interest to you and that match your academic focus. This will make the task more enjoyable and relevant:

News: Voice of America www.voanews.com/learningenglish/home/.

Lectures: TED.com at www.ted.com/.

Take note of words and phrases that are new to you. Write down any that you like and might want to use. Also, write down the ones you don't understand so that you can ask a tutor or friend for clarification. **Try not to get into the habit of simply skipping over words and phrases you don't know.** Take every opportunity to build your comprehension of academic English.

Note-taking skills

Accurate note-taking is an essential skill for classroom success. When you take notes on a video, lecture, or presentation, you must understand what the main ideas are. You also need to be able to distinguish the main ideas from the details, and the concepts from the specific examples.

Some students use a note-taking strategy that involves writing in two columns. The left column is main ideas, and the right column is supporting ideas or details. Listen for *signal words* and phrases like *such as* (which indicates that the speaker will give an example) or *at one point* (which refers to something from the past that is no longer current).

Another strategy is to use symbols and abbreviations, so you can write more quickly while you listen, but still record the main ideas and details you will need later when you review your notes.

Common Note-Taking Symbols

$	money
→	leads to, causes, results in
#	number
↑	increases, improves
↓	decreases, worsens
≠	is not equal to, is the opposite of

Common Abbreviations Used in Note-Taking

w/	with
w/o	without
inc.	including
i.e.	that is to say
e.g.	for example
etc.	et cetera, so forth
b/c	because
b/4	before
b/t	between
re:	regarding, about
esp.	especially
min	minimum
max	maximum
gov't	government
ASAP	as soon as possible
wk	week
mo	month
yr	year
vs.	versus, as opposed to
co.	company
ch	chapter
Q:	question
ex.	example
HW	homework
diff	difference

Speaking

Pronunciation

When you are multilingual, certain academic English sounds may be new to you and hard to produce. For example, English is one of the few languages that has the sound that is written as *th*. For many learning English, this is a difficult sound to produce consistently. In other cases, certain sounds may be similar to, but not exactly like, sounds in the other languages you speak. For example, the sound of the letter *R* in English is different from the sound of *R* in French. In addition to specific sounds, different languages have different rhythms and different intonations. They may also use vocal stress differently. These factors lead to what is sometimes called a *foreign accent*.

It is important for multilingual students to realize that it is not an appropriate or realistic goal to try to sound like a native speaker. In fact, unless you begin speaking English in an English-speaking society as a young person, it is highly unlikely that you will ever sound like a native speaker of that society. This is completely acceptable. **Ultimately, the goal of any speaker is that all listeners understand what is being said.** While you don't want listeners to have to make extra effort to understand you because of your pronunciation, grammar, or vocabulary, if people generally understand you, you should not consider your pronunciation a problem that needs to be fixed.

There is nothing wrong with a foreign or regional accent. Almost all universities have professors who teach with foreign and regional accents, and these professors are every bit as respected as any other professor on campus. If you do find yourself frustrated because people often cannot understand you, then you may want to take a pronunciation or accent modification class, work with a tutor, or use some kind of pronunciation software program to practice English. Conversation partners can also be a great help to you. This is simply someone you meet with regularly to chat, perhaps at a coffee shop or in a park. Talking with and listening to someone who has a great command of English pronunciation will be helpful to you. It is very helpful to know which sounds of English you are not producing clearly so that you can practice those specific sounds. Try to get some accurate feedback on this. Remember that pronunciation of a second or third language is basically an imitation process. Any time you listen to a native speaker of English—teachers, classmates, radio programs, television shows, films—you have an opportunity to listen to the sound of American English, which means more opportunities to imitate. Of course, some people are naturally better at imitating than others. Don't be self-conscious about asking for help with your pronunciation. Always remember that colleges are places of learning, and everyone who attends is interested in the learning process.

All students, multilingual and monolingual, who are preparing a public speaking project or a class presentation should make sure they know how to pronounce all of the words in the presentation ahead of time. If you are not sure how to pronounce a word, look it up, or ask a professor or a classmate. This is particularly important because presentations are often evaluated, at least in part, on the sound clarity of your pronunciation of academic English. Many online dictionaries now have a feature that allows you to hear how a word is pronounced. Take advantage of all the resources available to you as you prepare.

Fluency

Fluency refers to how well you can convey the ideas you want to, in the language you want to, at a regular speed, without having to pause or stop speaking while you think about vocabulary or grammar. The only way to gain fluency in academic English is to speak academic English. If you feel that you could be more fluent than you are, you need to put yourself in situations where you are speaking this way as much as possible. For some students, the time spent in class is the only time they are using academic English because at other times they are either alone or with other people who speak other languages and varieties of English. This is not the ideal situation for someone who wants to improve their fluency with academic English or any other language or language variety.

In addition to attending your classes and participating as much as possible, you can try these strategies for improving your fluency:

A. Don't just spend time outside classes with people from your home language group. Make friends, make lunch plans with, and form study groups with people with whom you will speak academic English.
B. Participate in extracurricular activities, such as sports, clubs, and volunteer organizations, with people who will be speaking academic English together.
C. Look for an internship at an organization in your field or area of interest where you can volunteer your time and use English in a professional setting.
D. If you are planning to work while you are a student, take a job where you will need to use formal English.

The way it works is this: The more academic English you speak, the more fluent you will become. Practice builds competence and confidence.

Public speaking and making presentations

Here are some things to keep in mind when doing any kind of spoken class presentation:

1. Make sure you have a clear introduction and a clear conclusion.
2. Don't speak too quickly. Try your best to keep your speed moderate.
3. Don't speak too softly. Make sure everyone can hear you clearly.
4. Stay energetic while you speak. If you speak with no energy, you will seem bored, and your audience will likely become bored. It's a good idea to move around a bit while you speak. Don't get stuck behind a podium for the duration of your presentation. Taking control of the space shows confidence and keeps audience members interested.
5. Make eye contact with members of your audience.
6. Try not to turn your back on your audience. Unless you have to write on the board or point out something with a visual aid, you should be facing the audience.

7. Make sure that your audience understands the vocabulary you are using. If you are using technical vocabulary or jargon that is only used within a particular field, explain what those terms mean as you use them.
8. Make sure that your spelling and grammar are correct in all written material you use in your presentation. For example, handouts, PowerPoint slides, charts, graphs, and maps should all be created using correct academic English. You don't want misspelled words or grammar errors on display for everyone to see! It will take away from your effectiveness as a presenter, and it will likely affect your grade negatively. If you need to use an intentionally misspelled word, put quotation marks around it, and explain it in your presentation to make sure your audience understands the point you are trying to make.

Treat presentations the way you would treat any writing assignment. Carefully go over everything you plan to say and display. Proofread, use spell-checking programs, and ask a professor or tutor to look over your materials beforehand.

TIP

If you are not sure about the pronunciation of any of the words in your presentation, make sure to find out *before* the presentation, and practice those words!

Reading

Academic English and the academic word list

Since the time that you started to learn English, you have encountered many different kinds of English. Some of these styles may have included journalism, fiction, and business English, as well as more day-to-day writing like the text you see in advertising and in website comments.

By now, you know that academic English is its own distinct variety of English. When you read academic texts, there is a certain kind of vocabulary you will need to understand in order to know what you are reading. For more on academic English, see "Using academic English" on page 18.

One way to become acquainted with the vocabulary commonly used in academic texts is to review the **academic word list.** This is a list of 570 "headwords" (the main form in a word "family"), which was compiled by linguist Averil Coxhead in 2000. Those 570 headwords are associated with 3,000 total words when you add in all the words in the word families. For example, the word *assist* is listed as a headword, and it is a common word in academic writing. These words are all listed as part of that family: *assistance*, *assistant*, *assistants*, *assisted*, *assisting*, *assists*, *unassisted*. To see the whole list, visit the academic word list website at www.uefap .com/vocab/select/selframa.htm.

As a helpful resource for self-study and practice with the academic word list, we recommend *Focus on Vocabulary: Mastering the Academic Word List* by Diane and Norbert Schmitt (Longman, 2005).

In order to understand the meaning of any unfamiliar words in the academic word list, or any words that you encounter in reading in general, you need a good dictionary. For multilingual students using English in U.S. colleges, it is always recommended that you use American English dictionaries in which the words and their definitions are given in American English. This is better than using translation dictionaries—it will ensure that you don't use the word in an incorrect way. We recommend the *Longman Advanced American Dictionary*, which comes with a CD ROM.

Affixes

Look at the word *unhelpful.* The first part of the word, *un-*, is a *prefix*. The meaning of this prefix is "not." The last part of the word, *-ful*, is a *suffix*. This suffix tells you that the word is an adjective. (The "help" part in the middle is called the root of the word.)

<u>u n</u> h e l p <u>f u l</u>
prefix suffix

Affixes (prefixes and suffixes) can help you with reading comprehension. Prefixes add meaning to a word, and suffixes usually tell you the word's part of speech. Once you are familiar with the meanings of different prefixes and suffixes, you have important information about a word whose full meaning you may not know.

Common English Prefixes

PREFIX	MEANING	EXAMPLES
non	not	nontraditional, nonsmoker
dis	"	disloyal, disagree
il	"	illegal, illogical
ir	"	irreversible, irrelevant
a	"	atypical, apolitical
*un**	"	uncomfortable, untalented
*in***	"	inconvenient, incomplete
**un* can also mean "opposite of"		undress, unlock
***in* can also mean "inside/into"		internal, insert

PREFIX	MEANING	EXAMPLES
anti (or *anti-*)	against	antibiotic, antiwar
auto	by itself	automatic, autobiography
bi	two	bicycle, bilingual
ex- (with hyphen)	former	ex-girlfriend, ex-president
ex	out of	external, exhale
inter	between	interoffice, intersect
micro	small	microchip, microscope
mis	wrongly	mistake, misunderstand
mono	one	monologue, monopoly
multi	many	multicultural, multinational
over	too much	overcharge, overreact
poly	many	polytechnic, polytheistic
post	after	postpone, postmodern
pre	before	predict, prehistoric
pro (or *pro-*)	in favor of	proponent, pro-choice
pseudo	false	pseudonym, pseudoscientific
re	again	rewrite, reconstitute
semi	half	semicircle, semisweet
sub	under	subway, subterranean
under	not enough	underpay, underestimate

- Note that **these prefixes do not always have these meanings** in every English word, but they can often give you a clue about a word's meaning.

- In front of a word beginning with *m* or *p*, the *in* prefix becomes *im*. Here are two examples: *immature*, *impatient*.

Following are some common English suffixes:

For nouns:

-tion/sion/ion	*-ity*	*-ness*	*-ment*
nation	unity	kindness	enjoyment
expansion	sensitivity	sadness	management

-ship	*-age/edge*	*-dom*	*-ery*
friendship	courage	kingdom	delivery
relationship	knowledge	boredom	scenery

-ance/ence	*-ism*	*-hood*
relevance	journalism	neighborhood
presence	communism	parenthood

- Common suffixes for "person nouns" are *–er* and *-or*: teacher, learner, player, writer, trainer, doctor, sailor, governor, professor.

For adjectives:

–y (added to a noun)	*-al*	*-ous*	*-ious*
windy	practical	famous	studious
icy	national	enormous	curious

-ful	*-less*	*–ic*	*-ive*
useful	useless	realistic	responsive
hopeful	hopeless	artistic	effective

-able	*-ible*	*-ary*
believable	edible	primary
comfortable	collectible	culinary

Four common suffixes for English verbs:

-ate	*-ize*	*-en*	*-fy*
celebrate	realize	weaken	electrify
educate	commercialize	soften	intensify

- Note that **these suffixes do not always mean that the word is the part of speech listed**, but as with the prefix list, knowing these patterns and tendencies can give you a clue about a word's part of speech.

Writing

Using academic English

In general, academic English differs from less formal English in the following ways:

1. Avoids using slang.
2. Uses formal words and sentences.
3. Uses standard grammar and spelling.
4. Uses specialized vocabulary related to specific fields of study.
5. Writers and speakers stay on topic and avoid lengthy sections that are irrelevant to the main point or that do not have a clear relationship to what has come before and what comes afterward.
6. Writers and speakers often share their point of view on a subject and exhibit critical thinking.

Here are some examples:

***Not* Academic English**	**Academic English**
He thinks the new laptops are totally cool.	He appreciates the innovations in the recently released laptop computers.
I'm gonna show you why that idea is stupid.	This paper aims to demonstrate the flaws in that plan.
Parents should go with kids who want help from the center.	Parents should accompany their children who seek assistance from the center.
The novel *Animal Farm* seems like it's about animals, but really it's about politics and the way bad leaders can make a crappy society.	The novel *Animal Farm* is an allegory for the way corrupt political leadership can engender a dystopian society.
B4 U go, pls call me.	Please call me before you leave.

When you write, you should always consider your audience. When you write for college courses, your professor will be the main audience for your writing. Just as it would be strange and inappropriate for you to write formally in a text message to your best friend, it would be unsuitable for you to write informally for most college classes. Your professors will be expecting you to use academic English.

Using thesauruses

A thesaurus can be a useful tool when you are writing in academic English. Thesauruses list synonyms—and sometimes antonyms—of words and can help you to vary your vocabulary and make it more sophisticated. For example, if you are writing about something that is big, a thesaurus will tell you that you could also use the words *enormous*, *gigantic*, or *mammoth*. These word choices may sound more academic and give your writing variety; however, you should be very careful with thesauruses because synonyms don't share the exact same meanings. There are always different shades of meaning, and these small differences will make the words you choose either appropriate or inappropriate for the contexts in which you use them. For example, a thesaurus might list the words *economical*, *thrifty*, *frugal*, and *stingy* as synonyms related to saving money or avoiding overspending. In fact, the first three words are commonly used to describe a positive characteristic, while *stingy* sounds negative and disapproving. Furthermore, a money choice can be described as *economical*, but not *thrifty*, which is used to describe a person or group. If the thesaurus does not explain these differences in meaning or use, look in a dictionary or search online for how these words are commonly used. A useful online resource is www.thesaurus.com.

Using discourse markers

Certain words and phrases, called *discourse markers* (or *transitional words* or *connectors*), are commonly used in academic English to clarify and organize the relationship between ideas in writing. It is important to know how and when to use these terms so that your reader is very clear about the relationships and so that your writing flows in a logical fashion. The words and phrases in **bold** below are examples of some effective discourse markers:

A. To introduce or get back to a topic:

With regard to the upcoming election, there are many different predictions.

Regarding the upcoming election, there are many different predictions.

As far as the upcoming election **is concerned**, there are many different predictions.

As for the upcoming election, there are many different predictions.

B. To show similarity in comparison:

Similarly, Hinduism is a polytheistic religion with multiple gods.

In the same way, Hinduism is a polytheistic religion with multiple gods.

Likewise, Hinduism is a polytheistic religion with multiple gods.

C. To show a contrast:

Some scientists, **on the other hand**, disagree that it is caused by pollution.

Some scientists, **on the contrary**, disagree that it is caused by pollution.

While some scientists believe it is caused by pollution, others disagree.

Some scientists believe it is caused by pollution, **whereas** others disagree.

Some scientists, **however**, disagree that it is caused by pollution.

D. To show a contradiction:

Heavy rain is predicted; **however**, we will go ahead with our hiking plans.

Heavy rain is predicted; **nonetheless**, we will go ahead with our hiking plans.

Heavy rain is predicted; **nevertheless**, we will go ahead with our hiking plans.

E. To add information:

This initiative would not help the community. **Moreover,** it would be very expensive.

This initiative would not help the community. **Furthermore,** it would be very expensive.

This initiative would not help the community. **In addition,** it would be very expensive.

This initiative would not help the community. **What's more,** it would be very expensive.

F. To show that something is a result of something else:

His book was highly critical of the government; **therefore,** it was banned.

His book was highly critical of the government. **As a result,** it was banned.

His book was highly critical of the government. **Consequently,** it was banned.

His book was highly critical of the government. **Hence,** it was banned.

His book was highly critical of the government. **Thus,** it was banned.

G. To introduce an example:

As an example, the blue whale has been on the list of endangered species since 1963.

The blue whale, **for example,** has been on the list of endangered species since 1963.

To illustrate, the blue whale has been on the list of endangered species since 1963.

Some animals have been on the list of endangered species for decades (e.g., the blue whale).

- Another simple type of discourse marker is the type that marks where the text is in *sequence*. Words like *first*, *second*, *third*, *next*, and *finally* are simple terms that can be very effective in keeping a reader's attention and making your writing well organized.

- The word *however* can indicate both a contrast (without a contradiction) and a contradiction. It has two different meanings in examples *C* and *D* above.
- There are other ways to use the terms used in the sentences above. If you're not sure, consult a grammar book or a tutor.

Using collocations

Collocations are word pairs that occur very frequently together in English, such as *wreak havoc* or *inextricably linked*. Your writing will come across as more fluent and natural if you use collocations. For a full discussion of this topic, see page 96.

Writing introductions and conclusions

Effective academic writing needs to have a strong introduction. Writers sometimes think of using a *hook* when they write an introduction. A hook is an interesting way to introduce your subject at the beginning of a piece of writing. A good hook makes a reader want to continue reading because it grabs his or her attention. A strong academic introduction usually also contains a clear statement of the main idea of the entire piece. This is called a *thesis statement*.

Conclusions are just as important as introductions. The conclusion should not end abruptly or introduce unrelated ideas. Instead, it should provide closure for your reader. Introductions and conclusions will be examined in more detail in chapter 3.

3

THE WRITING PROCESS

Modes of development

You will probably be asked to do many different kinds of writing in college. For example, you may write a lab report, a journal, an essay exam, a review of a campus event, a summary of an article, or a speech. One of the most common writing assignments you will have is the essay, in which you write about a particular topic. Your professor might give you an essay topic, or you may be asked to come up with the topic on your own. If you come up with your own topic, some professors will require you to get the topic approved. If you are not required to get topic approval, we suggest you still share your idea with your professor. In this way, you will know if your idea works well for the assignment.

Some professors teach different types of essays, such as *narrative*, *description*, *definition*, *exemplification*, *classification*, *comparison and contrast*, and *cause and effect*. These types of essays are commonly called *modes of development*. In writing classes, you may be asked to read and write these types of essays.

Most professors of composition, however, have moved away from these traditional modes and now focus mostly on *personal narratives*, in which you write about something personal, and *literacy narratives*, in which you write about your development as a reader and writer. Composition professors also tend to focus on writing *arguments*, in which you think critically about a topic and present an argument to your audience. Developing arguments will be examined in more detail later in this chapter.

A *research project* requires you to do research and use sources in your writing. Some research projects are *reports*, in which the writer gathers and presents information from sources on a certain topic. Others are *arguments*, in which the writer takes a point of view on a subject and uses research and supporting facts to help demonstrate why his or her point of view is the best or makes the most sense. If your instructor has assigned a research paper and you are not sure if it should be a report or an argument, then you should ask for clarification.

Prewriting

When you are given a writing assignment, you often have to come up with an interesting topic or angle that suits the assignment. This can be difficult for some writers. Some assignments will be very specific. For example, you might be asked to describe three differences between your home country and the United States. Other assignments will be open-ended. For example, you might be instructed to write an essay describing an event in your life that taught you something valuable. In both cases, it may be hard to know where to start. "What should I write about?" is a common question students ask when given a writing assignment.

There are several strategies you can use when you are trying to come up with a topic and generating ideas to go with that topic. These are often called *prewriting* strategies because they come before you write a full draft of your paper. It can be helpful to give yourself a time limit while you are prewriting. Five minutes is a good start. For example, you could challenge yourself to brainstorm or freewrite for a full five minutes before stopping.

It is important to remember not to edit or proofread as you prewrite. Editing and proofreading are very important steps in the writing process, but they should be saved for later. At the prewriting stage, it doesn't matter if you spell words correctly or write complete sentences. You are simply trying to generate as much information as possible. You should resist the urge to waste time editing during your prewriting. You wouldn't want to spend time rewriting something that may not even become part of your essay.

Following are some prewriting strategies you can try. Remember that not every strategy will work for every writer, and not every strategy will work for every writing project. Try them all to find the ones that work best for you.

1. *Brainstorming* is often the first prewriting strategy used by writers. When you brainstorm, you list all of the words and phrases that come to mind about your topic. You don't need to write whole sentences, and it doesn't matter if some of the ideas seem silly or irrelevant. You write down everything you can think of, and then you can go back, look over what you have on your list, and circle the ideas that seem like they are worth more consideration. You may also notice relationships between some of the words or ideas that can be explored further.
2. *Freewriting* often comes after brainstorming because you can take an idea you came up with during brainstorming and use it as the topic of your freewrite. When you freewrite, you write steadily without stopping. You write everything that comes to mind. The writing may be disorganized and unfocused, and some of the sentences may be incomplete, but you try to let the writing flow, rather than creating a list like you do during brainstorming. If you freewrite without stopping for at least five minutes, you will generate a lot of ideas. When you have finished, you can go back and pick out parts that you think would be good to put in your paper or develop further.
3. *Looping* means looking into your freewriting and pulling out a phrase or a sentence and then using it to begin another freewrite. You can continue to loop back to your original freewrite, or you can create loops from your loops! Prewriting is messy, and it is important to try out these techniques and make them work for you.
4. *Researching* a topic can also help you find an angle for your paper. If you are asked to use sources in your assignment, reading what has already been written about the topic can be very helpful. You will see how your thinking fits with what has already been discovered. Books, library databases, and websites are good sources to consult. If you are not sure how to use these sources, ask a librarian or your professor for

help. Even if you are not required to use outside sources, you may still want to familiarize yourself more with a subject by reading about it before you start writing. For more about using sources, see "Using sources" on page 41.

5. *Talking* with people can also be helpful when you begin a writing project. Conversations about your topic with people who are experts on it or at least have ideas or opinions about it may lead you in an interesting and even surprising direction.
6. *Outlining* often comes after you have generated ideas, done research if necessary, and have a good idea about how your paper will go. When you outline, you organize the parts of your paper into a list. This is often thought of as a blueprint for your paper. Some writers always work with outlines, and others don't. Complex projects may be difficult to organize without an outline, and you may find that simple projects don't really need an outline. Again, find what works for you.

Drafting

If you make an *outline* of the structure and main ideas you plan to write about, you can refer to it as you begin drafting your essay. If you don't start with an outline, you may want to write a *discovery draft* and then go back and organize your thoughts into an outline. Either way, you do need to make sure your final drafts are well organized.

There may be times when you are asked to write a five-paragraph essay. This can be a useful organizational strategy when you are writing a short essay or for an in-class exam, but it can also be a very limiting structure. It certainly won't work when you want to fully develop complex ideas and include numerous examples to support your point of view. The five-paragraph essay structure may come in handy as a starting point for longer projects. When you do need to write more fully developed papers, you can turn each of the three paragraphs of the five-paragraph essay into sections that include multiple paragraphs each, and you can add as many sections as you need. When you do this, your ideas will be more fully developed, and you won't have to worry about meeting page-length requirements because the pages will accumulate easily.

Let's imagine you have been asked to write a five-paragraph argumentative essay of the type shown on page 36. The five-paragraph essay requires that you come up with a main idea for your essay, which is called a *thesis statement*. It is typically included at the end of the introduction. Then, you will need to include three ideas that support that main idea. These ideas will make up the three *body paragraphs*, and finally, your essay will need a *conclusion*. As an example, let's say that your instructor has asked you to choose a current world trend and write about your view of that trend. That is a large topic for only five paragraphs, but with careful planning, you will be able to produce an organized essay that presents your point of view.

After brainstorming for five minutes and freewriting for ten minutes, let's say you choose globalization as your topic. Now, you need to make sure you have a solid understanding of what globalization really is. Once you fully understand it, you need to decide what your point of view on this trend is. Do you support it? Are you against it? Do you have mixed feelings? Does it depend on which aspect is being discussed? You need to think critically about your topic.

Suppose that you read a few articles, talk to some friends, check out some information online, and then decide that globalization is generally beneficial. Now, you need to come up with three ideas to support that view, each of which will be suitable for a paragraph. A rough outline might look something like this:

Globalization

Intro/thesis:	It's mostly a good thing because it benefits people economically, socially, and culturally.
Body paragraph #1:	Globalization brings economic benefits.
Body paragraph #2:	Globalization brings social benefits.
Body paragraph #3:	Globalization brings cultural benefits.
Conclusion:	Globalization is inevitable, and that's O.K. because it's good.

- Notice that each of the three ideas presented in the thesis are presented in the same order in the body paragraphs. When you list the points in the thesis that correspond to the body paragraphs, you have written what is known as a *blueprint thesis*. You do not have to write a blueprint thesis, but if you do, readers will expect you to follow that organizational pattern throughout your essay.

- You may choose to present your strongest point first to grab your readers' attention and convince them of your point of view early on, or you may choose to present your strongest point third so that your readers are left with the most important point at the end.
- Writing the body paragraphs first, and the introduction and conclusion last, is a good strategy because you may not know how to introduce and conclude your writing until the body paragraphs are completed.
- As you write, make use of the discourse markers mentioned in chapter 2. It is important for you to be a good guide for your readers.
- Keep a record of all sources you plan to cite. You must have the exact information for your citations. See "Quoting" on page 42 for more information on using quotations.

Revising, editing, and proofreading

Once you have written a full draft, you should read through the paper to see what parts are clear and what parts need more work. Are there ideas that need to be more fully developed? Have you made your point of view clear? Are the points presented in the best order? Does the introduction do a good job of pulling readers in, and does the conclusion do a good job of providing closure? When you work on improving these *higher order concerns*, you are revising.

In addition to reviewing your paper yourself, it is helpful to get a professor, tutor, or classmate to review your work. It is important to find out how an impartial reader will receive your writing. You are writing for an audience, so it is appropriate to test it out on real people. You will gain valuable information from them regarding how well you have conveyed your intended meanings.

When you go back and make changes based on the areas you and your reviewers have pointed out as needing work, you are revising. *Revising* is an essential step and usually takes the most time during the writing process. It is important to be open to change while you are revising. Be careful not to get too attached to specific parts of your writing. Remember that your ultimate goal is to create the best paper possible, and you must do what it takes to achieve this. This may mean removing a section that took you a considerable amount of time to write, and it may mean that you have to add a section you weren't counting on adding. Writing is hard work, but it is worth it because, in the end, you will have clearly conveyed your ideas to an academic audience.

Once the paper has been revised several times, and you believe the ideas and the organization are in good shape, it is time to review the paper for *lower order concerns*. When you look for lower order concerns, you focus on *editing* sentence-level issues, such as grammatical, punctuation, and vocabulary errors. You also work on *proofreading* for mistakes with spelling, capitalization, and typos, as well as missing words, wrong words, and other surface problems.

- If you already know that you have a tendency to make certain kinds of mistakes (for example, misuse of articles, or misuse of commas), **it is a good idea to do a special review in which you only look for that type of mistake** (for example, look at all the articles or all the commas, or look out for all of the places where you may have missed an article or comma.)
- Another technique that some writers use is **reading each sentence in the paper in the reverse order**. When you do this, you read the last sentence first, and then, you read the sentence above it, and so on. This will allow you to focus on the spelling, punctuation, grammar, and vocabulary of each sentence without being distracted by the content.
- It may also be helpful to **read your paper out loud** to yourself. This helps some writers to find their errors. For example, if you read your work out loud, it may be easy to see where you have left a word out. For people who are new to English, reading aloud may shift your attention to pronunciation, which is a different skill. If this is true for you, it may be more helpful for you to ask someone else to read your paper out loud to you. It will be helpful for you to see where the reader stumbles or has trouble understanding what is written.

Making an argument

Much of the writing you do in college will require you to have a clear point of view, in other words, an *argument.* Argument, used in this sense, is not about people disagreeing or fighting with each other; it is about taking a firm stance on an issue and persuading your audience that your stance is correct.

As mentioned earlier in this chapter, when you write your argument essay for an academic audience, you will be expected to clearly and succinctly state your argument in a thesis statement. The thesis statement should be presented in the introduction, and since it is the main idea of the entire essay, the writer is expected to *support the argument* clearly, logically, and as persuasively as possible throughout the essay. You should not include points in your essay that do not pertain to your argument. You should stay focused on your argument the entire time.

What makes a good thesis statement?

A thesis statement presents an argument that people can reasonably argue for and against.

- If you simply present a fact, such as "Barack Obama is the forty-fourth president of the United States," there is nothing to argue. This is not a good thesis statement.
- If you present something that most people would never argue against, such as "People should not steal from other people," then you do not have a good thesis statement. The same goes for statements that most people would never argue for.

In addition to making a clear argument, a good thesis statement should present a justification for the side you are taking. Here is an example of a good thesis statement:

> "Laws against sagging pants should be repealed because they aim to take away the civil rights of American citizens."

There are two sides to this argument, which were presented on page 5. The statement makes it clear which side the writer is taking, and people could reasonably argue for and against the statement.

Finally, the statement does a good job of providing a *justification* for the writer's argument. You can still disagree with the statement, but the writer has explained why he or she is making the argument.

Some people like to think of an umbrella when they think of a thesis statement. All of the main ideas in the essay should further the argument of the thesis statement. If certain key ideas in the essay are not "covered" by the umbrella, either you don't have a good thesis statement, or the idea should be removed from the essay because it is not relevant to the thesis statement.

Argumentative writing involves making *claims* and providing *support* for those claims. If you are writing a research paper on global warming, for example, and you claim that global warming is harmful for the planet, you need to provide support for that claim in the form of examples and facts. Your support will help your readers to understand why you made a claim, and your support should help to convince your readers to agree with your claim. Remember, too, that the support you provide must be valid. Valid support can come from reliable sources, but if you aren't using outside sources in your paper, it should still be based on sound reasoning.

Two ideas that are often a feature of this academic, argumentative style of writing are concession and refutation. A *concession* is when the author presents an opposing opinion. Imagine that a writer's main thesis is that a certain plan proposed by the mayor is a good plan. He might start off a sentence this way:

> "While it is true that some citizens of our town may not directly benefit from the plan..."

In this sentence, you can see that the writer is *conceding* that there are weaknesses in the plan, but the writer will go on to explain why his or her stance that it is a good plan outweighs this negative fact.

A *refutation* is when the author claims that the opposing opinion is not valid, reasonable, or credible. The second part of the sentence below presents a refutation:

> "While it is true that some citizens of our town may not directly benefit from the plan, the majority of citizens will benefit, so the plan should be put into action."

Concessions and refutations are good techniques to use in argumentative writing because they strengthen the writer's argument by showing that the writer is aware of all sides of the issue. This makes the argument seem more valid.

Writing an essay

Five-paragraph academic essay format

The boxes below show how to format a standard five-paragraph academic essay. Remember, this is not the only way to organize an essay, but it is an approach that is considered acceptable by many professors, and it is a good format to follow if you are not sure how to begin.

Paragraph 1 = Introduction

- Begin with a hook that will grab your reader's attention, such as a fact, definition, quote, statistic, historical reference, anecdote, or rhetorical question.
- Clearly introduce your topic and prepare readers for what is to come in the essay.
- End with a clear and succinct thesis statement.
- The introduction starts broad and ends very focused. That is why it is depicted with a point at the end.

Paragraph 2 = First Body Paragraph

- Begin with a topic sentence that states the main idea of this paragraph.
- The main idea should clearly support the thesis statement.
- Give specific examples and details that clearly explain the idea and support the thesis.

Paragraph 3 = Second Body Paragraph

- Begin with a topic sentence that states the main idea of this paragraph.
- The main idea should clearly support the thesis statement.
- Give specific examples and details that clearly explain the idea and support the thesis.

Paragraph 4 = Third Body Paragraph

- Begin with a topic sentence that states the main idea of this paragraph.
- The main idea should clearly support the thesis statement.
- Give specific examples and details that clearly explain the idea and support the thesis.

Paragraph 5 = Conclusion

- Restate the thesis one last time for readers.
- Wrap up the essay in a logical way.
- End with a quote, summary, call for action, intention, or prediction.
- The conclusion starts very focused on the thesis and ends broad. That is why it is depicted with a point at the beginning.

Make sure each paragraph is well developed with examples and details. One way to make sure you develop your writing is to "show" instead of "tell."

Telling is when you simply make a statement, such as

"I worked hard."

Showing is when you use details that really paint a picture for your readers, such as:

"I spent a solid week reviewing the materials, drafting a budget, and writing the formal proposal. I was at the office every evening until 10:00 p.m., and I never took a break for lunch. At the end of the week, I met with the leaders of the group to make a formal presentation. I was exhausted by the weekend, but it was worth it because the proposal was approved."

In these sentences, the writer never actually states, "I worked hard," but you understood this because of the information provided. Showing is more interesting for readers because it provides much more information. It will also make your writing longer, so you won't have to worry about meeting minimum word or page requirements. When you write a research paper, you can "show" by including more facts and sources to back up your points. When you write personal narratives, you can "show" by adding descriptive language.

Discussion of terms

1. A *hook* is an interesting way to introduce your subject at the beginning of a piece of writing. A good hook grabs a reader's attention and makes the reader want to continue reading.
2. A *fact* is something known to be true. For example, you could begin an essay about China's economy by stating: "Over 1.3 billion people live in China. This population figure is greater than that of any other country on Earth." This is an example of a fact that is common knowledge, so the source is not necessary. If the fact you use is *not* common knowledge, you should cite the source. For example, you would need a citation if you wrote, "Florida produces about 75% of the U.S. oranges and accounts for about 40% of the world's orange juice supply" (State of Florida.com).
3. Beginning your introduction with a *definition* may not be the most exciting hook, but it is often an appropriate way to get started, particularly if the easy will use a term that represents a complicated idea or an idea unfamiliar to your readers. For example, if you are writing about a technical subject, and your readers need to know the meaning of a term to understand everything that follows, you might choose to define it first. In an essay about the concept of risk homeostasis, you

might begin this way: "Risk homeostasis refers to the theory that, in systems, if risk is identified and reduced, then a different element of risk will increase elsewhere in the system."

4. A *quote* is often a good hook. Be sure to cite all quotes you use.
5. A *statistic* is a useful way to introduce an essay. For example, you could begin an essay about global warming by stating, "The United States contributes 25% of atmospheric emissions despite the fact that it constitutes only 5% of the world's population" (elawreview.org). You must cite the sources of all statistics.
6. A *historical reference* is an effective way to hook your reader if something from history relates to the main topic of your essay. For example, if your essay is about modern-day Alaska, you could start with something like this: "According to Lockard (2011), 'At various times a wide Ice Age land bridge connected Alaska and Siberia across today's Bering Strait, and the evidence for a migration chiefly from Asia over thousands of years is strong' (p. 12)." After this, you would need to link this opening idea with your thesis about modern Alaska so that by the end of the introduction, the thesis has been reached in a clear and logical way.
7. An *anecdote* is a real story that happened to you or someone else that somehow relates to or illuminates some point about your essay topic. For example, if your essay is about World War II, you could start by writing, "My grandfather enlisted in the Italian army in 1941, and the experiences he had in the next few years permanently shaped the kind of person he became." Funny anecdotes can also be effective and set a light-hearted and entertaining tone to an essay.
8. A *rhetorical question* is a device whereby a writer uses the format of a question, as a writing style choice—not to ask for an answer, but to make a statement or raise an issue. For example, in an essay on world hunger, you might start with a rhetorical question like this: "In developing countries around the world, millions of children do not have enough food to eat. Is this the kind of world we want to live in?"
9. A *call for action,* which is a good way to end a conclusion, is a suggestion that a writer makes about what someone needs to do in order to solve some problem or improve a situation. For example, in an essay in support of a political initiative for

improving public education, you might end this way: "Everyone in the state of New York must call, write, and email our representatives to urge them to support the proposed education plan; our children cannot lose out on the education they deserve."

10. An *intention* is a writer's stated plan to do something related to the thesis of his or her essay. For example, in an essay about a student's own language learning, she might end by saying, "In the end, I realize that the only way my English will reach the level that I want to achieve is if I continue to focus on vocabulary learning, push myself to speak as much as possible in class, and write in my journal every day."
11. A *prediction* is a writer's speculation about the future. It is an effective and logical way to end a piece of writing about a contemporary issue. For example, in an essay about immigration policy, you might write, "Unless we change the immigration policy and fix its flaws, both the United States and the skilled people who wish to join it will continue to lose out."

Sample argumentative essay

The following is an example of a five-paragraph argumentative essay. It is written in APA style. See the comments in the right-hand margin for further information about the vocabulary and style.

Globalization: A Welcome Trend

Title gives an indication of the main thesis of the essay.

This morning, I woke up, walked over to my Ikea desk, and checked the Internet to see what was happening around the world. Then, I got a ride to class in my roommate's Volkswagen Passat. On the way, I called my friend on my Nokia cell phone and told him I'd meet him later for lunch. After class, we had a delicious Turkish lunch of shish kebabs and baklava. I did some studying in the library, and then, I went to my taekwondo class. Later, my classmates and I went to see the new Hayao Miyazaki anime film that everyone is talking about. At the end of the day,

Begins with a personal **anecdote** to hook the reader.

it occurred to me how different my life is from the life my grandparents had, largely because of globalization. We all have an idea of what globalization is, but sometimes, it is difficult to define it precisely. One comprehensive way to think about globalization is as the exchange between countries of trade, finance, information, culture, and ideas. For some people, the increase of globalization represents one of the best aspects of modern life. Others, however, view globalization as a negative trend. Those who feel that globalization has detriments which outweigh any benefits are not looking at the big picture and seeing this trend for what it actually is. In fact, globalization is a positive trend with the potential to enrich everyone's life and contribute to people's well-being—economically, socially, and culturally.

Academic word meaning "all-inclusive, including everything."

Discourse marker *however* used to show contrast clearly.

Academic word meaning "bad side," or "negative aspect."

Idiom that means "the complete/entire situation."

Thesis statement, which has a clear point of view and summarizes the controlling idea of the entire essay.

Some critics say that globalization leaves the poor behind and only affects those in rich countries, but this is not completely accurate. Those people might point to the fact that globalization allows foreign investors to take advantage of workers in developing countries by paying low wages. They might also say that competition from foreign countries drives down the prices of locally manufactured or grown products, which decreases income for the poor. The reality is much more positive, however. Advocates of globalization, such as economists and business leaders, maintain that increased international trade leads to economic growth, which is good for the poor as well as the wealthy. They point out that international

The first topic sentence introduces the "economic benefits" idea with a **concession** (stating the opposing opinion) and a **refutation** (refuting that opinion).

More concession.

More refutation.

Instead of repeating the verb say, he uses the **reporting verbs** *maintain, point out,* and *argue* in this paragraph.

competition leads to innovation, and the result is better products which all of us can use, and more efficient processes in areas like manufacturing. Consequently, certain products become cheaper and easier to afford for everyone, including the poor. Advocates also argue that when a country experiences economic growth, it is linked to an expanding middle class. This means that people previously ranked as "poor" can be lifted up into a more prosperous segment of society, and their standard of living improves. As an example, according to the United Nations (2009), China's middle class grew from 65.5 million people in 2005 to 80 million people in 2007. The UN linked this growth directly to China's economic growth as a result of increased globalization. They observed a similar trend in India, where globalization-fueled economic growth is expected to expand the middle class from about 5 percent to more than 40 percent of the country over the next two decades.

In addition to the economic benefits, there are social benefits to globalization. Increased trade and globalization can facilitate political reforms by expanding the freedoms that ordinary citizens have and giving them more control over their lives. An article in *Business Week* observed that "democracy and globalization are clearly linked because countries that are more open to international capital flows are also more likely to offer political rights and civil liberties to their citizens" (Sittel, 2010, p. 29).

Discourse marker *consequently* is used to show result.

Academic word that means "rich."

Specific example is provided for support with a discourse marker.

Legitimate, credible source is used for statistics, with full citation in the list of references at the end.

Example of an APA style in-text citation when the author is mentioned in the sentence, and there is no page number.

Another specific example is provided for support.

The second topic sentence introduces the "social benefits" idea. It includes a transition statement, makes the flow of the essay better by clearly linking paragraphs 2 and 3 with a discourse marker.

Academic word which means "make easier," or "make more likely."

Legitimate source used for support. Full citation listed in references at the end.

APA style in-text citation.

The article presents the case of Indonesia where the economic and financial opening-up of the country made it more difficult for autocratic governors to maintain the control they had before, resulting in increased democratization. In developing countries, expanded markets mean people have more access to the items they need and want for their lives and businesses. This in turn can reduce corruption, as there is less need to depend on or bribe government officials. Less political corruption means a better society.

Finally, the cultural benefits of globalization cannot be denied. Some critics of globalization place undue focus on the proliferation of chain stores and restaurants which make towns and cities around the world more uniform. Others contend that globalization of culture is basically Americanization of culture and that the United States is saturating the rest of the world with Coca-Cola, Hollywood movies, American music, and the English language. Again, this viewpoint fails to take in the larger picture. Japan is one example. Japanese culture has very successfully been imported into the United States and other countries. Sushi has become a familiar, commonly available treat. Western kids from all walks of life enjoy Nintendo and Sony video games and love trading Pokémon and Digimon cards. They read manga comics and watch anime films. Their parents go to karaoke bars with coworkers after work. Meanwhile, the lives of people in Japan may

Specific example is provided for support.

Academic word meaning "having unlimited power."

The writer concludes the paragraph with a strong statement that is difficult to dispute.

The third topic sentence introduces the "cultural benefits" idea and uses the **discourse marker** *finally* to remind the reader where we are in the sequence of ideas.

Academic word meaning "too much," or "inappropriate."

Academic word meaning "rapid spread/increase."

Another good **reporting verb** that substitutes for *say*.

Academic word meaning "filling completely."

Here, the writer once again makes a concession and then a refutation.

Idiom that means "different backgrounds and social groups."

Many specific examples given.

be enriched by award-winning dramas from Mexico, comedies from France, and exciting Hong Kong action movies. Music lovers everywhere can enjoy the Latin-flavored pop of Spain's Enrique Iglesias and Colombia's Shakira. People in city parks can be seen practicing capoeira, the dance-like martial art from Brazil. As for the spread of English as the world's language, this should be seen as a good effect of globalization. The more we can all communicate with each other, the better we will understand each other and get along. English does not really "belong" to Britain or America anymore, if it ever did. It's the language of globalization.

Discourse marker to introduce an idea.

Those who have a negative view of globalization are focusing on the wrong aspects of this phenomenon. Once all of the effects of this trend are examined together, the picture is clear. Globalization makes all of us, as a world community, richer, freer, and more cultured. We can take the best of what we have to offer and send it around the world, and our fellow citizens of the world can reciprocate by doing the same. Globalization allows everyone to experience the best of what is available. As former UN Secretary-General Kofi Annan once said, "Arguing against globalization is like arguing against the rules of gravity."

Restatement of the main idea in slightly different terms.

Academic word meaning "to do something because something similar has been done to you."

Ends the conclusion with a quote that supports the main idea. Source of the quote is listed in the references.

References

BrainyQuote. (2011). Kofi Annan quotes. Retrieved from www.brainyquote.com/quotes/authors/k/kofi_annan.html

Sittel, H. (2010, April 9). Democracy and globalization. *Business Week*, *135*, 28–31.

United Nations. (2009, October 13). Middle classes grow in China and India. Retrieved from www.un.org/en/

All sources cited in text should be included in the reference list. Do not include any sources in the list if they were not cited in the text. The reference list should begin on a new page.

Arrange sources in alphabetical order.

Abbreviate the first name of an author.

An organization can be an author.

In the reference list, APA style requires capitalizing the first word of a title, proper nouns in a title, and the first word in a title after a colon. It does not capitalize other words in a title.

Using sources

Writing that uses sources is different from other kinds of writing in several important ways.

Here are a few issues to keep in mind when you use sources for academic writing:

1. Legitimacy of the sources
2. Quoting
3. How to cite the sources
4. How to paraphrase
5. How to avoid plagiarism

Let's look at these issues one at a time.

Legitimacy of the sources

When we talk about the *legitimacy* of sources, we are talking about how accurate, truthful, and appropriate they are for academic writing. In academic writing, it is important that the facts, quotations, statistics, and other similar pieces of information that you use be accurate. One way to make sure the information is accurate is by using only reliable, credible sources. Blogs and online wiki sites such as *Wikipedia* are generally *not* good sources for academic writing because you can't always be sure who is writing the information, which means you won't know the author's credentials. You also won't know whether or not the information is exaggerated, distorted, or simply not true. In contrast, materials that have a clear author and have been published by a publishing company are much more likely to be accurate and viewed as legitimate sources. This includes books, magazines, newspapers, and scholarly academic journals—either the kind you can physically hold and read or the ones retrieved from an online database. There are some websites that professors and other readers of your work will consider to be legitimate. Examples of these might include government websites, websites for nongovernmental organizations (NGOs), and museum websites.

TIP

If you are not sure if a source that you might use in your writing is legitimate, ask your professor for help.

Quoting

A *quotation* is the **exact words** someone else has spoken or written. Often, the shortened version of this word—*quote*—is used. A famous quote from Dr. Martin Luther King, Jr. is "I have a dream today."

The word *quote* can also be used as a verb: we have just *quoted* Martin Luther King Jr. Some styles of writing may not have any quotations in them, such as a personal essay on an aspect of your own life. Other styles often use a lot of quotations, such as a research paper for a psychology course. Meaningful and appropriate quotes can enhance a paper. How can you decide whether or not to use a quotation in your paper? Maybe someone has written or said something that uses language in a particularly interesting way, for example, in a catchy, appealing, or original manner. Maybe they have stated an idea in a way that you consider to be powerful. Maybe their quote provides persuasive support for your thesis. In such cases, you might want to use that quote.

The writer of the sample argumentative essay chose the Kofi Annan quote to end his paper: "Arguing against globalization is like arguing against the rules of gravity." This is an effective quote because:

A. It uses language in an interesting way. This quote uses a literary device called a *simile* to compare globalization with gravity.
B. It was said by an authoritative person relevant to the topic. Kofi Annan is the former head of the United Nations.

If the quote you are planning to use does not serve one of the functions above, or it does not in some way support the thesis of the paper, it will likely be a bad choice for an academic paper. A quote from, for example, a pop singer such as "Globalization is happening now," would not add anything to the paper because it does not use interesting language, the speaker is not an authoritative source on the topic, and it does not back up the writer's thesis that globalization is a positive trend. It simply states that it is happening.

Although quotes can be effective, you don't want to overuse them. Most of the writing in your paper should be yours. If you have too many quotes, your professor may think you are too dependent on other sources and may not think you have developed enough of your own ideas. You can check to see if you have too many quotes by highlighting all of the quotes in your paper. If you don't have much left of substance once the quotes are removed, your paper is out of balance. Your challenge will be to make sure you are developing your ideas in your paper and using meaningful quotes only to support the ideas you have developed.

How to cite sources

To *cite* a source means to mention or list it in your writing, to let the reader know where you found certain ideas, information, or quotations. It is important to cite sources accurately. When you cite sources, **anyone who reads your work should be able to find the exact sources you used.** If a reader is not able to do this, you may not have cited your source correctly. Sources can be mentioned in the main part of an essay or paper (*in-text citations*), in *footnotes* or *endnotes*, or in a *bibliography*.

The two formats most commonly used for citing sources in U.S. college writing are **APA style** and **MLA style**. Other formats sometimes used include Chicago Style, AMA, and Turabian. *MLA* stands for Modern Language Association, and *APA* stands for American Psychological Association. Usually, an instructor will tell you which format to use for an assignment. If the professor has not specified a style, you should ask for clarification. MLA style is most commonly used in the humanities, such as literature and art. APA is more commonly used in the social sciences: it is often called the *author–date style* because it places both right in the text in the form of *in-text citations*. It is a useful style to use when the timeliness of your sources is important. For example, if you were writing a research paper on a health issue, it would be important to see right in the text how current your sources are.

An example of an in-text citation using APA style would be something like this, with authors and publication year given:

Johnson & Takeshita (2007) have demonstrated that local economies don't always benefit more from government loans.

An example of an in-text citation using MLA style would be something like this, with author and page number of the publication given:

Gabriel Garcia Marquez is "the father of the Latin American magical realism style in the popular imagination" (Fernandez 117).

Notice that the first example is called a *paraphrase*, while the second one is a *direct quote*. More is said about paraphrasing on page 46. A direct quote in APA would also require a page number, and all direct quotes require quotation marks.

Some writers use *footnotes* or *endnotes* in their work. Footnotes and endnotes have a small number written after the section in your text that you are commenting on. They can be can be used to provide extra information, background, or clarification to your writing, and they can also be used to cite sources.

When they do cite sources, they sometimes refer the readers to the specific pages of the sources listed in the bibliography. The small number after the text in your paper refers to a same-numbered comment somewhere else. Footnotes are written numerically at the bottom of the same page where the source has been used. Endnotes are written in numerical order at the end of a paper or book on a separate page titled "Endnotes."

Here is an example of a footnote:

As Fernandez has noted, Gabriel Garcia Marquez is "the father of the Latin American magical realism style in the popular imagination."[1]

The reference footnote appears at the bottom of this page.

If you are not sure if you should use footnotes or endnotes in your writing, ask your professor. The complete information for all of the sources you have used in your writing commonly comes at the end of the paper you have written, in the form of a list. Sometimes this is called a *bibliography*. In APA, it is called *References*, which means it includes only those sources that are referred to in the paper. In MLA, it is called *Works Cited*, which means it only includes those works that are cited in the paper. Some formatting styles and some professors allow lists of *Works Consulted*, which include all of the sources you consulted during the project, even if you didn't actually cite them in the paper. This is rare, so check with your professor before attempting to create a list of works consulted.

An example of a source listed in an APA-style "References" section would be something like this:

Johnson, R. & Takeshita, F. (2007). The effect of local government loans on the economies of small communities. *Journal of Economics, 150,* 250–265.

An example of a source listed in an MLA-style "Works Cited" section would be something like this:

Fernandez, Diego. *Magical Realism in Latin American Fiction.* New York: Simon and Schuster, 2001. Print.

[1]Diego Fernandez, Magical Realism in Latin American Fiction (New York: Simon and Schuster, 2001) 117.

Always ask your professor which kind of citation format is required and follow that format carefully. We suggest you consult the Purdue University's Online Writing Lab (OWL) for help learning how to cite sources using APA and MLA formats. It is an excellent resource. The web address is www.owl.english.purdue.edu/. You should also consult your professor and campus tutors for help. Keep in mind that these styles are often updated, so you should always refer to a guide to make sure you are adhering to the most recent rules.

How to paraphrase

Paraphrasing is an important skill to have when you do any kind of academic writing.

Paraphrasing means using your own words to explain or refer to someone else's idea or quotation. As an example, here is a sentence you might encounter in a book:

"The annual tuition charged by different universities cannot reasonably be seen as reflective of the value of the education offered by each institution." – Edward Gulley

You might not feel that you need to quote this directly because there is nothing especially catchy or powerful about the language, but you may want to add this idea to your paper. In this case, you could paraphrase it like this:

As researcher Edward Gulley points out, there is not necessarily a correlation between a university's tuition and the value of the education that it provides to students.

When you paraphrase, you should use your own words without changing the intended meaning of the original source. Your paraphrase should contain all of the ideas in the section being paraphrased, and it should not add any ideas that were not in the original section being paraphrased. If you use words from the original source, especially several in a row, it will look like plagiarism, unless you enclose them in quotation marks. An exception to this would be certain technical terms that are always written with the same vocabulary.

Sometimes, paraphrasing involves summarizing a large amount of information from someone else's work rather than rewording a specific piece of text. Here is an example of a summary:

Based on ten years of detailed research, Edward Gulley has concluded that students often do not know what to expect from the college experience and that they later regret some of the choices that they have made (Gully, 2009).

When you paraphrase or report on something someone else has said or written, you can make your writing more varied and more sophisticated if you use *reporting verbs* instead of repeating the word *say* (or *write*). Here are some examples:

In his 2010 paper, Professor Tolbert *wrote* that the structures are not identical.

In his 2010 paper, Professor Tolbert *explained* that the structures are not identical.

In her speech, the CEO *said* that her products were completely safe.

In her speech, the CEO *maintained* that her products were completely safe.

Following are some common reporting verbs:

A. When someone says something that is **not a main point:**

Anna *pointed out* that it would be difficult to finish the project by Thursday.

added
indicated
mentioned
remarked
commented
stated
told (us)
made the point
suggested
brought up

B. When someone wants to really **emphasize or highlight a point:**

The prime minister *insisted* that there was no other solution to the crisis.

stressed
emphasized

C. When someone wants to really emphasize a **point of view or opinion:**

John *contended* that his book was the best textbook for our class.

declared
claimed
asserted

D. When that opinion is being given a bit **defensively** (it may be challenged or opposed):

Alexandra *held* that it was her book, not John's, which would be the best choice.

maintained
argued
protested
countered

E. When someone states something reluctantly (something that **they would rather not state**):

The manager *acknowledged* that the department had made some mistakes.

conceded
admitted
confessed

F. When someone **gives an answer:**

The assistant *answered* that she did not know when Maria would return from vacation.

replied
responded

G. When someone provides a **guess** or says something **unproven:**

The students *guessed* that the teacher was not feeling well.
theorized
speculated
hypothesized

The students *predict* that the teacher will feel well tomorrow.

H. When someone wants to communicate a **possible bad result:**

The officer *warned* that the park is not a safe place after dark.
cautioned

I. When someone gives a **suggestion** (note how the verbs are used below):

The professor *advised* us to study for the test.
urged

She *advised* that we study.
suggested
recommended
proposed

J. Other verbs with very **specific meanings:**

- The teacher *announced* that there would be a test.
- Carlos *promised* that he would finish the project by Thursday.
- The old man *exclaimed* that Jill looked exactly like his ex-wife.
- Ms. Hensen *specified* that she only wanted the strawberries if they were ripe.
- The engineers *concluded* that the heat had been a factor in the accident.
- The prisoner *denied* that he had committed the robbery.
- Sandy *explained* that she had been away from the office for two weeks.
- Toshi *repeated* that he did not want to be the one to tell Sheila.
- The salesman *implied* that the car might be too expensive for our budget.

How to avoid plagiarism

Plagiarism (pronounced "plā-jə-ri-zəm") is a very serious offense in American academic institutions and must be avoided. It occurs when you use someone else's exact words, ideas, or images without indicating that you have done so. Academic institutions dictate that student writers must give credit to their sources. It is up to you to make sure you have done this correctly. If you want to use someone else's words or ideas in your writing, there are two ways to avoid plagiarism:

A. Enclose the word-for-word material in quotation marks and properly cite the source.
B. Paraphrase the material and properly cite the source.

TIP

In your academic writing, your readers will expect anything that is not clearly attributed to a source, and not common knowledge, to be *your own ideas, your own words, and your own sentence structures.*

Now that it has become so easy to find information on the Internet and "cut and paste" it into a document, plagiarizing is tempting for stressed-out (or lazy) students who are struggling to meet a deadline. Keep in mind, however, that professors know how to find plagiarized material and may even use an online plagiarism detection program. Furthermore, a professor can often identify writing that is not yours because parts or all of the paper either do not seem to go together, or the writing is different from what you have turned in previously. Your professor will become familiar with your "voice" as a writer and will be able to recognize when the writing you are turning in is not yours.

Plagiarism in academia is about using either someone else's words or someone else's ideas. When we say "ideas," we mean academically oriented hypotheses, predictions, research results, conclusions, analyses, and observations of similarities and differences. We are not referring to what would be considered common knowledge. If you write that "nutritious food is good for your health," for example, you don't need to provide a source because it is considered common knowledge. If, however, another writer has noted that the increase of manufacturing in one Chinese city has directly led to the decrease in a neighboring city, and you mention this idea in your paper, you must cite the original author, as this would not likely be common knowledge.

Remember that **unintentional plagiarism** is still plagiarism. You are always responsible for the work you submit for a grade. It is your responsibility to make sure your sources are properly credited according to the style guidelines you are following. Students who do plagiarize may fail an assignment, fail the course, or be expelled. Even if something might not be considered plagiarism in another country, it will be considered as such if it goes against the rules for American academic institutions, and students will have to accept the consequences. Excuses such as, "I didn't know this was considered plagiarism," or "I didn't know that plagiarism is wrong," or "I'm a foreign student," will not help you.

TIP

When you take notes from sources, be very careful to record exactly where you got the material so that you can cite it accurately.

4

English Language Support

Top Ten most common errors made by multilingual students

Following is a list of common mistakes multilingual students make in writing. Details about how to address each issue are also provided.

1. Misuse of articles
2. Misuse of prepositions
3. Wrong verb tense
4. Wrong part of speech
5. Misuse of uncountable nouns
6. Run-ons and fragments
7. Misuse of commas
8. Misuse of conditional forms
9. Inaccurate use of vocabulary
10. Translating directly from native language

Let's look at these in more detail:

Misuse of articles

There are three different kinds of errors pertaining to articles:

1. Missing article: This is ^ very important issue for my country.

2. Wrong article:

   There are three reasons for this: one is economic,

   the
   another is political, and ~~an~~other is cultural.

3. Extra unneeded article: Many people in ~~the~~ Korea are interested in changing this.

As with other kinds of writing errors, if you receive feedback that you are making different kinds of mistakes with articles, try to identify patterns of errors that you can look out for as you write. For example, if you know you have a tendency to omit articles, read through all of your written work looking just for the places that need articles, and add them. This is the strategy presented in chapter 3. For additional information on articles, see "Articles" on page 93.

Misuse of prepositions

Like articles, languages use prepositions differently, which makes them hard for learners to master in English. As an example, English speakers say, "She is married **to** a lawyer," "I worry **about** my problems," and "I can count **on** my friends." Spanish speakers, on the other hand, when speaking Spanish, say, "She is married **with** a lawyer," "I worry **for** my problems," and "I can count **with** my friends." This fact makes accurate preposition use a tricky goal for all language learners.

One useful strategy is to memorize common verb–preposition combinations (e.g., believe in) and adjective–preposition combinations (e.g., married to). Many English grammar books will have such lists in their appendix. Here is one such list:

Common Preposition Combinations

With VERBS:	With ADJECTIVES:
apologize for	absent from
argue with	addicted to
arrive at	afraid of
approve of	angry with (someone)

With VERBS:	With ADJECTIVES:
believe in	angry about (something)
blame for	aware of
complain about	bored with
communicate with	capable of
consist of	concerned about
cope with	connected to
contribute to	covered with
deal with	deprived of
depend on	disappointed in (someone)
deprive of	disappointed about (something)
empathize with	divorced from
sympathize with	dressed in
escape from	due to
fight for	excited about
focus on	familiar with
forget about	filled with
hide from	grateful to (someone)
hope for	grateful for (something)
look forward to	guilty of
participate in	hooked on
pray for	interested in
provide with	involved in
rescue from	jealous of
say to	known for
stop from	limited to
succeed in	married to
take advantage of	opposed to
take care of	patient with
talk about	pleased with
think about	polite to
vote for	prepared for
worry about	prohibited from
	protected from
	proud of
	qualified for
	related to
	responsible for

With ADJECTIVES:
satisfied with, scared of, thankful to (someone), thankful for (something), upset with, used to

These verbs do <u>not</u> usually take any preposition directly after: assure, contact, convince, discuss, handle, inform, manage, persuade, remind, teach, tell, visit

Another strategy is to use a search engine to find examples of English sentences on the Internet that use the words you want to use and see which prepositions are being used. For example, if you want write about jealousy, type in "he is jealous him" in your browser, and you will see many examples where the word *of* comes after the adjective *jealous*. This can be helpful, but remember, not everything you find on the Internet can be trusted, so talking with a professor or tutor is also helpful.

Wrong verb tense

See pages 72–78 for more information.

Wrong part of speech

See pages 59–63 for more information.

Misuse of uncountable nouns

See pages 64–67 for more information.

Run-ons and fragments

A. A *run-on* sentence is a sentence that needs to be shortened for style reasons or punctuated differently for grammar reasons. The common type has two independent clauses connected incorrectly.

> A **clause** is a phrase with a subject and a verb.
> An **independent clause** can stand alone as a complete sentence:
>
> We went home. There is a lot of traffic.
> John is coming later. It's raining.

> A **subordinate (dependent) clause** cannot stand alone as a complete sentence:
>
> Because it was late.
> So I'll have to put on my coat.
> Even though it's morning.

Here is an example of a run-on sentence:

Carol is the best student in the class (independent clause #1) she gets an *A* on every test (independent clause #2).

To correct it, you could make them into two different sentences:

Carol is the best student in the class. She gets an *A* on every test.

You could also choose to add a comma and a conjunction such as *and*:

Carol is the best student in the class, and she gets an *A* on every test.

A semicolon could also be put between the clauses because the clauses are closely related:

Carol is the best student in the class; she gets an *A* on every test.

A semicolon has the feeling of a period but is used to closely connect clauses by keeping them in the same sentence.

Another specific kind of run-on sentence is called a **comma splice**. This occurs when a writer puts a comma between two independent clauses, which is a mistake:

We want to travel to Mexico in September, my sister lives there.

To correct this, you could choose one of the same three options mentioned above: make this two sentences, use a conjunction (here the word *because* would make sense), or replace the comma with a semicolon.

B. A *fragment* does not have all of the elements it needs to be a complete grammatical sentence.

Common Examples:

No subject:	Is really easy to learn to cook.
No verb:	It so late that we had to finish working and go home.
No subject or verb:	For example, many different kinds of food.
No independent clause:	Because it was so expensive. Although it was raining. Without knowing how to solve it.

To correct a fragment, you need to know why it is a fragment and rewrite the sentence adding in the missing element.

Misuse of commas

The following are four common areas where students are likely to make mistakes with commas:

A. In sentences with **comma splices** (see page 56).

B. **With nonrestrictive adjective clauses** (see page 85).

C. **After subordinate clauses.** If a subordinate clause begins a sentence (followed by an independent clause), it must have a comma after it:

Because she was late, we had to wait for her.
^

Although they are twins, they look fairly different.
^

Whenever Mary walks in the rain, she gets a cold.
^

D. **Before coordinating conjunctions.**
The coordinating conjunctions in English are:

for, and, nor (meaning "because")

but, or, yet, so (meaning "but")

The comma rule: If there is an independent clause with a new subject after the coordinating conjunction, you usually need a comma:

> I like baseball**, and** all of my brothers like it also.
> ^
>
> We wanted to go to the park**, but** it was too cold.
> ^
>
> We realized that we had two choices; we could go to the movies**, or** we could stay home.
> ^

Misuse of conditional forms

See page 89.

Inaccurate use of vocabulary

It's good to try to use new words in your writing to expand your vocabulary, but sometimes you may receive feedback that you used an English word the wrong way. When this happens, make sure you understand why you used it the wrong way. Perhaps the word is part of a *collocation* that you don't know, or perhaps it is *not* a common collocation with the other words you used with it. (For more about collocations, see page 96).

Also, maybe the word is only used negatively or positively, or only to describe people, or never to describe people. If an instructor or reader tells you that you used a word the wrong way and you are not sure why, ask for clarification.

Translating directly from native language

Notice how strange and unnatural this sentence sounds: "As for the party, did you like it?" However, if you were to you translate it into Japanese, it would sound natural and correct. We know that different languages use not only different words, but different word structures and grammatical phrasing. If English is a second language for you, it is not a good idea to write something in your native language and then translate it into English. For one thing, the English may sound unnatural; the sentences may have structures that don't sound like English. Also, you may be tempted to use translation dictionaries too much, which could result in inaccurate translations of words and phrases.

Remember that very often a common idiom in one language sounds strange or makes no sense in another. In English, the idiom "I was beside myself" means "I was upset." Now translate "When I lost my job, I was beside myself" word for word, into your native language. Does it make sense? Does it sound natural? It probably does not.

Additionally, sentences that have an appropriate length in one language may, when translated, seem too long. This can often be true, for example, with sentences translated from Spanish to English. **You should write in English using the English vocabulary and sentence structures you know and by imitating good English writing.**

Grammar and vocabulary use and practice exercises

In this section, certain basics about standard American English grammar and vocabulary are reviewed. While you may know much, or all, of the information here, think of it as a reference to consult while you are writing if you are unsure about anything.

Parts of speech review

Nouns

- Words for a person, place, thing, or idea
  friend, forest, desk, happiness, information
- Includes proper nouns (names)
  Harvard University, Barack Obama, Brazil
- Some nouns are abstractions (you cannot touch them)
  love, kindness, peace, luck, hope
- Nouns can be **countable** or **uncountable**
  one bottle, some shampoo; two suitcases, some luggage

- Some concepts have both a "person noun" and an "idea noun"
  communicator, communication; lawyer, law; immigrant, immigration

For a list of common suffixes on English nouns, see page 17.

Verbs

- Action words about doing something
  work, talk, see, call, write, cancel, crash
- **Stative verbs** about existence, emotions, thought, etc.
  be, understand, cost, mean, belong
- Four common suffixes for English verbs are *-ate*, *-ize*, *-en*, *-fy*
  celebrate, industrialize, strengthen, electrify

For more on stative verbs, see page 81.

Adjectives

- Words that modify (tell more about) nouns
  big, yellow, important, understandable
- Includes **participial adjectives** with *–ed*, *-en*, *-ing*
  completed, broken, interesting, interested
- Includes **quantifiers** ("amount" words)
  many, several, few, three, one hundred
- Includes **hyphenated** (two-word) **adjectives**
  old-fashioned, hard-working, long-lost

For a list of common suffixes for English adjectives, see page 17.

Adverbs

- Words that modify verbs and adjectives
  very, quickly, suddenly, well, loudly
- Tell when, where, how, how much, how often
  often, never, soon, here, really, occasionally
- Most English adverbs end in the *–ly* suffix
  carefully, softly, intelligently, finally

Irregular Adverb Forms: Some adverb forms are irregular. Here are the most common ones. When you are writing, keep these forms in mind, and make sure you are using them correctly.

ADJECTIVE	ADVERB	
good	well	She did a good job. She did it well.
fast	fast	She is fast. She runs very fast.
hard	hard	He gave a hard push. He pushed it hard. (not *hardly*)
late	late	It is late. They arrived late.
early	early	It is early. They came early.
daily	daily	Daily exercise is good. She exercises daily.
difficult	with difficulty	The test was difficult. He did it with difficulty.

A special note about *easy* and *easily*: *easy* (adjective) means "not difficult," and *easily* is the adverb form; it is not irregular. Make sure you are using these words correctly. They don't mean "common" or "often."

correct: "The mountain climb was <u>easy</u> for her; she <u>easily</u> climbed it in one hour."

incorrect: "It is <u>easy</u> to see people eating noodles in my hometown." (This is not the best word; *common* is better.)

incorrect: "You can <u>easily</u> see people using cell phones these days." (This is not the best word; *often* is better.)

The opposite of *easily*, as listed above, is *with difficulty*.

Pronouns

- Refer to/substitute for nouns
  I, you, he, him, this, it, whose, their, they, us

Prepositions

- Words about time, direction, place
  in, out, at, of, on, for, with, about, under

Conjunctions

- Connecting words
  and, but, or, although, because, however

Interjections

- Convey emotion
  wow!, oh, ouch!, hey! oops, aha!

Articles

- Introduce nouns
- Definite: *the*
- Indefinite: *a, an*

See page 93 for a more detailed description of article use in English.

PRACTICE 4A: Parts of Speech

What part of speech is each word in these word families? Circle one.

	Noun	Verb	Adjective	Adverb
1. know	N	V	Adj	Adv
2. knowledge	N	V	Adj	Adv
3. knowledgeable	N	V	Adj	Adv
4. knew	N	V	Adj	Adv
5. electronic	N	V	Adj	Adv
6. electric	N	V	Adj	Adv
7. electrification	N	V	Adj	Adv
8. electrify	N	V	Adj	Adv
9. electricity	N	V	Adj	Adv
10. electrical	N	V	Adj	Adv
11. success	N	V	Adj	Adv
12. successful	N	V	Adj	Adv
13. succeed	N	V	Adj	Adv
14. successfully	N	V	Adj	Adv
15. photographer	N	V	Adj	Adv
16. photography	N	V	Adj	Adv
17. photographic	N	V	Adj	Adv
18. photograph	N	V	Adj	Adv
19. strong	N	V	Adj	Adv
20. strongly	N	V	Adj	Adv
21. strength	N	V	Adj	Adv
22. strengthen	N	V	Adj	Adv

23. health	N	V	Adj	Adv
24. healthy	N	V	Adj	Adv
25. healthily	N	V	Adj	Adv
26. healthful	N	V	Adj	Adv
27. heal	N	V	Adj	Adv

Circle the correct part of speech from the underlined choices:

28. One of the best things about my sister is her amazing <u>creative</u> <u>create</u> <u>creativity</u>.
29. I think a nice flower garden can really <u>beautifully</u> <u>beauty</u> <u>beautify</u> a house.
30. My brother is very <u>success</u> <u>succeed</u> <u>successful</u> in his job at the bank.
31. My parents are <u>opposition</u> <u>oppose</u> <u>opposed</u> to my sister's boyfriend.
32. These days, the <u>economy</u> <u>economic</u> <u>economize</u> of China is getting stronger and stronger.
33. Gun control is a <u>controversy</u> <u>controversial</u> <u>controversially</u> issue in my state.
34. I agree with the mayor that we must <u>improved</u> <u>improve</u> <u>improvement</u> the public schools in our town.
35. I feel very <u>connection</u> <u>connected</u> <u>connector</u> <u>connect</u> to my older brother.

Some common irregular plural forms

Usually, to make a noun plural, you add *s*. Here are some of the most common nouns that are exceptions to that rule and have irregular plural forms.

Never add *s* to the irregular plural form (e.g., *childrens*).

<u>**Singular**</u>	<u>**Plural**</u>
man	men
woman	women
child	children
person	people
foot, tooth, goose	feet, teeth, geese

mouse, louse	mice, lice
ox	oxen
leaf, wife, knife, loaf, shelf	leaves, wives, knives, loaves, shelves
wolf, half, self, thief, life	wolves, halves, selves, thieves, lives
die *(noun: used in games)*	dice

Also:

Certain words borrowed from Latin language. For example:

syllabus, nucleus, stimulus	syllabi, nuclei, stimuli
curriculum, addendum	curricula, addenda

Certain words borrowed from Greek language. For example:

thesis, crisis, analysis	theses, crises, analyses
diagnosis, hypothesis	diagnoses, hypotheses
phenomenon, criterion	phenomena, criteria

These words have no change in plural form:

fish, moose, deer	fish, moose, deer
offspring, series, species	offspring, series, species

Uncountable nouns

(Also sometimes called *noncount nouns.*)

Many common English nouns are uncountable, which means the following:

1. You cannot add a **plural *s*** to them.
   He says a lot of *truths.* (WRONG)
2. You cannot use the word ***many*** in front of them.
   They played many nice *musics.* (WRONG)
3. You cannot use ***a*** or ***an*** before them.
   I have a nice *jewelry.* (WRONG)
4. You cannot put **a number** before them.
   She gave me two *informations.* (WRONG)

It's useful to think of this as a grammar idea more than a vocabulary idea or meaning idea. It is not always clear to English learners, just by the meaning, that a certain word is uncountable.

Here are some examples:
The word *suitcase* is countable. → "two suitcases," "many suitcases"
The word *luggage* is uncountable. → "some luggage," "luggage"
(Not "two luggages" or "many luggages," even though the meanings of *suitcase* and *luggage* are very similar.)

Examples of common uncountable nouns:			**certain categories:**
advice	music	homework	**liquids** (e.g., wine, shampoo, gasoline)
garbage	jewelry	work	**gerunds** (e.g., speaking, smoking, boxing)
information	furniture	junk	**materials** (e.g., wood, gold, cotton, steel)
energy	equipment	news	**sports** (e.g., soccer, baseball, tennis)
traffic	staff	stuff	**subjects** (e.g., biology, literature, journalism)
architecture	clothing	vocabulary	**abstractions** (e.g., happiness, peace, friendship)
electricity	mail	slang	
heat	makeup	money	**weather words** (e.g., snow, rain, wind, thunder)
truth	research	luggage	**things with small pieces** (e.g., sand, salt, rice)

TIP

When you are writing, if you are not sure if a noun you are using is countable or not, check it in a dictionary.

Here are some other tips:

- To make uncountable nouns countable, grammatically, you can put a countable noun in front of them.

a glass of wine	a cube of ice
a piece of equipment	a grain of sand

- The word *piece* often works.

- Uncountable nouns are singular nouns that take singular verb forms:
  The equipment is broken.
  Salt costs less than sugar.
  The news was good.
- Instead of *many*, with uncountable nouns you can use *a lot of*, *lots of*, and forms of *much*:
  a lot of homework
  lots of wine
  so much traffic
  too much rain
  not much energy
- The word *clothes* is unusual. It is uncountable, but sounds fine with *many*, and takes the plural form:
  A lot of clothes are expensive.
  She has many clothes.
  (Not "a clothes," or "five clothes.")

  For the singular countable form, you say "a piece of clothing." (Not "a piece of clothes.")
- Many nouns have a countable meaning *and* an uncountable meaning, depending on how they are used:

Examples:

Countable	Uncountable
A glass of wine	Some glass
Many times	A lot of time
There are three spaces left on the list.	We don't have enough space for a piano.
I caught so many fish in the lake.	He doesn't eat fish.
Broccoli is a healthy food.	There's not much food at this buffet.

PRACTICE 4B: Countable and Uncountable Nouns

Identify the mistakes with countable and uncountable nouns below and correct them.

1. I want to learn formal vocabularies in English class, not just slangs.

2. That teacher is good, but he gives too many homeworks!
3. One hundred is too much dollar to carry in your pocket.
4. How many time do I need to tell you? We don't have enough times to stop for coffee!
5. If you eat more vegetables, you will have more energies!
6. Professor Kennedy has good advices about studying; you should get some suggestions from him.
7. Where can I buy some equipments and furnitures for my new home office?
8. Marlene packed so many clothes for the trip; she must have at least 50 clothes in her suitcase!
9. I need some informations about the researches your hospital has done on heart disease.
10. I have never seen snows or frozen rains; we don't have those weathers in India!

Non-referential it

In the phrases that follow, the pronoun *it* is not actually taking the place of, or even directly referring to, a noun. Instead, ***it* is serving as the subject** in these sentences because full English sentences always need subjects. This use of *it* is sometimes called the "empty it."

It's raining outside.

It is always busy here on Fridays.

It takes a long time to make a chocolate cake.

Be aware of the "empty it" in your writing. If you sometimes make errors with this structure, review all of your sentences for just this error before you hand in a piece of writing for the professor to review.

PRACTICE 4C: Non-Referential *It*

Correct these sentence errors related to the non-referential *it*.

1. Is so cold here in the winter.
2. There is so fun to go to Disney World.
3. Maria thinks is going to be a really fun party.
4. We need to get ready for the ceremony because is almost 2:00!

5. At dinner in my house, difficult to hear because people talk so loudly.

Modal verbs

Modal verbs, sometimes just called *modals*, are words that appear before verbs and express an attitude about something.

Following are the modals:

can	will	may	should	must
could	would	might	ought to	

The structure for *all* modals is:

MODAL + BASE VERB

A modal does not have the same meaning in different sentences, and its meaning can change depending on the context. Here are the common uses of modals in the present:

1. **Polite request**: using *could, can, may, might, will, would*
   Can you turn out the lights, please?
   Would you please pass the salt?
   May I see your photos?

2. **Necessity / prohibition**: using *must, must not, may, may not, cannot*
   (Also the **phrasal modals** *have to* and *have got to* listed below.)
   You must register for the class before you can take it. You have to do it online.

   You may not smoke in class. You can't smoke in the hallway, either.

3. **Ability**: using *can, cannot*
   I can speak Spanish, but I cannot speak French.

4. **Advisability** (advice): using *should, ought to; shouldn't, ought not to*
   You should pay more attention in class. You ought to study more.

5. **Future possibility**: using *might, may, could; might not, may not (***but not** *could not)*
   It may rain tomorrow. It could even snow. It might be a good idea to bring a coat.

6. **Future simple tense:** using *will*
   I will finally finish the semester tomorrow. Then we'll have a party.

7. **Assumption or certainty**: using *might, may, could, should, ought to, must, have to,* plus *not* for negative forms. The degree of certainty changes a bit with these words:

Dan is in the library.	→	Absolutely certain
Dan **has to/must** be in the library.	→	Sounds somewhat certain
Dan **should/ought to** be in the library.	→	Sounds less certain
Dan **could/may/might** be in the library.	→	Sounds like the speaker is not sure
I don't know where Dan is.	→	Uncertain

Additionally, **phrasal models** are two- and three-word phrases that are used like modals:

have to	(= "must," no choice)	You have to leave right now!
have got to	(= "must," no choice)	We've got to leave now! It's 1:00 a.m.
had better	(= "should" with a implied consequences)	You'd better study, or you'll fail the test!
supposed to	(= what is expected)	You're not supposed to smoke in here.
would rather	(= preference)	I'd rather take physics than chemistry.
would like to	(= "want," "desire"—the polite form)	Would you like to have more cake?
going to	(= used to show future, intentions)	I'm going to call Karen after class.

Modals in the past tense

Grammar structure of modals used in the past tense:

MODAL + *have* + past participle

↥ base form

This structure is also called *modal perfect*:

You should have seen the game last night!

He must have left already; I don't see him now.

She might have given him his birthday gift early; I'm not sure.

If it is a negative statement, the word *not* goes in between the modal and *have*:

You should not have come. It was a bad idea.

He must not have left. There's his coat.

Often, in less formal writing styles, these forms are contracted: for example, *should've*, and *mustn't have.*

Here are three common kinds of modal perfects for past ideas:

1. **Regret:** using *should, ought to; shouldn't, ought not to*

   I should not have eaten all that candy!

   You ought to have helped him.

2. **Possibility:** using *may, might, must, could, would, have to; may not, must not, could not, would not, cannot* (but not *can*)

   He cannot have known the plan since he was absent.

   He may have seen it.

   You could have called your sister! Why didn't you?

   Ming cannot have spoken to Wen yet; it's only 4:00 a.m. in Beijing.

3. **Conditional result:** using *would, could, might; would not, could not, might not*

   If I had not been so tired, I would have stayed longer. I might have seen you!

For more on conditional sentences, see page 89.

Other uses of modals in the past (**not** modal perfects):

4. **Past habitual:** using *would* or *used to* (as a phrasal modal) + base verb:

   In 2009, I would walk to work every day.

   I used to smoke. I don't anymore.

5. **Form-changing past phrasal modals**

   Some phrasal modals change form in the past tense:

   have to + base verb becomes
   had to + base verb → "I had to get a vaccination to travel to Tanzania."

   be going to + base verb becomes
   was/were going to + base verb → "I was going to call you, but it got too late."

6. **Modals not used in the past**
   Some modals are not used in the past at all. We do not usually use *can*, *will*, *had better*, or *must* to express past ideas.

must, like *have to*, becomes *had to* in the past

<u>Present</u>		<u>Past</u>
"We must take the test."	→	"We had to take the test."

PRACTICE 4D: Modals

Identify errors with modals in the sentences below, and then correct them.

1. I must have to go to English class now.
2. If you go to China, you may get a visa beforehand.
3. It can rain tomorrow.
4. When you swim underwater, you might come up to breath air.
5. Jonathan must be in the bathroom right now; I'm not sure.
6. I was have to go to see my dentist yesterday, so I missed the class.
7. Erin musted to pick her kids up from school, so she couldn't come to the concert.
8. You should not took the money, which did not belong to you.

9. I saw the movie today; Paul might saw it yesterday.
10. Marcy was used to drink coffee every morning, but she stopped.

Verb choice problems

Present simple versus past simple

Present simple tense is used for facts (facts that are true now) or habits, or routines:

We both <u>like</u> pizza.

Carl <u>works</u> as a lawyer.

I <u>remember</u> the year 2008. (I remember it now. This is a true fact about the present).

Chinese cooking <u>uses</u> a lot of noodles.

Andrea <u>is</u> happy that she got a promotion at work. (She is happy now. This is a true fact about the present).

Words and phrases like *always, often, usually, every day, each morning, once a week, in the wintertime,* etc., can signal a habit or routine, which requires simple present tense, even if some of that behavior happened in the past:

Ellen often <u>goes</u> skiing with her family.

I usually <u>avoid</u> walking in the park after dark.

Sarah <u>calls</u> her mother each morning.

Once a week, we <u>eat</u> at my grandparents' house.

Simple past tense is used for things that happened in the past, at a certain time in the past, and are now finished or over. It is often used with a past time word or phrase such as *yesterday, five minutes ago, last week, in 2007, at that time, when I was younger, when she was in college,* etc.:

Ellen <u>went</u> skiing with her family last year.

I <u>avoided</u> walking in the park last night.

Sarah <u>called</u> her mother this morning.

At that time, I <u>was</u> a college student.

If you use simple past to describe people or their habits and routines, it could imply that they are dead:

> President Reagan had brown hair.
>
> My grandmother liked ice cream.

Remember, you can mix tenses in one piece of writing. Here is an example:

> The TOEFL test is very hard. That's why I was so nervous when
> fact (now) past event
>
> I took it. I usually study hard for tests. When I had to take the
> past event habit past event
>
> TOEFL test in 2008, I studied harder than ever. I remember this
> past event fact (true now)
>
> very well! I got a good score, and I feel proud about that.
> past event fact (true now)

PRACTICE 4E: Verb Tenses

Circle the best tense choice for each sentence.

1. When I was in college, I swim / swam every day.
2. My neighbor is traveling to California next week, and she is / she was really excited.
3. This past weekend, my cousins and I play / played video games for hours.
4. Devon was so excited when he sees / saw his name on the list of students accepted into the program.
5. I went to the wrong class because I think it's /thought it was Tuesday, not Wednesday.

The present perfect tense (versus present simple and past simple)

The *present perfect* tense sometimes causes difficulty for nonnative English speakers because other languages may not have this verb tense, or they may use it differently.

The basic idea: Present perfect is not like the past (finished), and it is not like the present (now). It usually refers to something that **started in the past but also affects "now."**

We do not use it with specific times in the past or with things happening right now. We use it to relate past actions to "now."

It is formed with the auxiliary verb *have* or *has* plus the past participle form:

	Have/Has + Past Participle		
I	have	walked	seven miles today.
She	has	seen	many movies.
All of us	have	known	Beth for four years.
The teacher	has	taught	at this school before.

Some common, specific uses of the present perfect tense include:

1. **Experience:**

   I have lived in Rome and London. = I am a person [now] who lived in those cities [in the past].

   Scott has never studied French. = Scott is a person [now] who did not ever study French [in the past].

2. **Result (now) from a past action** (sometimes called *present result*):

   You have lost a lot of weight! = You are thinner [now] because of exercise and diet than you were [in the past].

   Patrick has passed all of his exams! = He's successful [now] because of his test performance [in the past].

3. **Recent action (so recent that it affects "now"):**

   I have eaten lunch already. = I am someone now who just ate lunch [in the recent past].

   We have decided to get married! = We just got engaged [in the recent past].

4. **Repetition of an activity in the past** (can be similar to "experience"):

   Ahmed has received three promotions at work. = repetition of job promotions in the past.

   We have met many people from Korea here. = repetition of meeting people from Korea in the past.

IMPORTANT RULE: **Remember that we never use the past perfect with specific times in the past!**

Correct: I have seen all of the *Star Wars* movies. (an experience idea)

Correct: I saw all of the *Star Wars* movies last year on DVD. (simple past tense is needed)

Incorrect: I have seen all of the *Star Wars* movies last year.

TIP

These adverbs are often used with the present perfect:
ever, never, already, yet, since, so far

PRACTICE 4F: Present Perfect tense

Which of the two underlined choices is perfect tense? Circle it.

1. Have you ever taken / did you take a physics class?
2. We have decided / we decided to move to Paris!
3. Last month, Linda has walked / walked six miles home from work.
4. In 2001, my uncle has died / died after a long illness.
5. How many times have you visited / did you visit New York City since you moved to Boston?

Progressive verb forms

Progressive verb forms always use a form of *be* plus the present participle (*-ing* form of the verb).

Examples:

I am studying. **I was studying.** **I will be studying.**

They are different from the **simple tenses** because they focus on an **action in progress** or the **duration** of an action. Use these forms when you want to show that an action is in progress, was in progress, or will be in progress.

Correct: I am working on my essay right now.
Incorrect: I work on my essay right now.

Correct: The rain was coming down very hard when we first met.
Incorrect: The rain came down very hard when we first met.

Correct: When you call me back, I will probably be hanging out with George.
Incorrect: When you call me back, I will probably hang out with George.

Present perfect progressive tenses (with a form of *have* + a form of *be* + the present participle) are used to focus specifically on the **duration of an action,** so there is a (direct or implied) time period.

I have been studying for a long time.

I had been studying (for two hours) when you came to see me.

I will have been studying at Harvard for three years when you finally move back to Boston.

IMPORTANT RULE: **Never use stative verbs with progressive forms.** **See page 81 for more on this rule.**

Future verb forms

There is no specific verb form in English to convey the future (as there is in some other languages). Here is a list of the common ways to express the future in English:

1. ***will*** **and** ***be going to***

   The most common way to express future in English is the **future simple** (*will* + base verb), or with *be going to* + base verb.

   Use ***will*** **+ base verb** for a **future fact** or **willingness** or **a decision/intention made at that moment:**

   I will turn 30 this year. (fact)

   Will you help me? (willingness)

   The phone is ringing; I'll get it. (intention made at that moment)

   Use ***be going to*** for **intentions, future plans,** and **decisions (not made at that moment).**

   I'm going to sign up for that class. (intention)

We're going to get married this spring. (future plan)

When Jasper grows up, he is going to be a scientist. (intention/future plan)

I decided that I am going to try to learn Chinese. (decision)

TIP

In casual speech, "going to" is sometimes pronounced "gonna," which is slang—there is no such word. You should never write "gonna" in academic writing.

In some cases, *will* and *be going to* convey the same meaning.

Basic future idea:

He will finish the project tomorrow.

He is going to finish the project tomorrow.

Prediction:

I think you will do well on the test.

I think you are going to do well on the test.

2. **Present progressive** is sometimes used to express **near future** and **arrangements.**

   I'm leaving for Europe tonight.

   She's going out at six o'clock.

   We are meeting on Thursday.

3. **Simple present** is sometimes used for **timetables** or **schedules.**

   The train departs at 9:00 p.m.

   The show is on television in one hour.

4. **Future progressive** is used to show an action in progress in the future:

   Don't call us at eight o'clock because we will be eating dinner.

5. **Future perfect** compares two future events and shows which one comes first (often with *by*):

   By 2011, I will have studied here for one year.

   She will have finished her degree already when you visit her.

6. **Future perfect progressive** is used to emphasize the duration of a future perfect idea, often with a time phrase:

   By 2011, we will have been studying here for a long time, almost five years!

7. ***About to*** means something that will take place in the **very near future:**

   I am about to call my friend. (in five seconds)

8. **Adverbial time clauses (subordinate clauses) in the future use simple present tense:**

When	Tom calls, we will tell him the news.
As soon as	she arrives, we will leave for the party.
Before	we celebrate Christmas, we will have our house party.
After	winter is over, we will plant the new flowers.
By the time	I go to New York, Eun will be back in Korea.

   Do not use *will* twice in these sentences. ("As soon as she will arrive..." is wrong.)

9. **The verbs *plan, intend,* and *hope,*** when used in the present, are about the future:

   I plan to go to medical school next year. I intend to be a doctor, and I hope to be successful.

PRACTICE 4G: Future Verb Forms

Which of the two underlined forms is better? Circle it.

1. If you need someone to get more milk, I'm going to / I will do it.
2. Lexie and I decided that we're going to / we will get some ice cream after class.
3. The flight to London is about to depart / departs at ten o'clock tonight.
4. As soon as I will get / get the information, I will tell it to you.
5. Anna will come see us after her seminar is / is going to be finished.

Phrasal verbs

A phrasal verb is a two-word or three-word verb. For example:

to *figure out*
to *get rid of*

You often cannot guess the meaning of an unfamiliar phrasal verb, even if you know the meaning of the individual words (that is, they are usually *figurative*).

to look = to see with your eyes.
up = a direction, towards the sky.

But, *to look up* (phrasal verb) = to research something, to find facts (in a book or on the Internet).

Phrasal verbs are extremely common in spoken English. You may have difficulty understanding casual speech or film and TV dialogue if you do not know common English phrasal verbs, but they are also used in academic English.

When a phrasal verb takes an object afterward, there are two types of patterns: *separable* phrasal verbs (the object can go **in between** the two words), or *inseparable* ones, where the object **must go at the end** of the two words.

Separable	Inseparable
correct: I called **Bruce** up.	**correct:** I got over **my problem.**
correct: I called up **Bruce.**	**correct:** I got over **it.**
correct: I called **him** up.	**incorrect:** I got **my problem** over.
incorrect: I called up **him.***	**incorrect:** I got **it** over.

***IMPORTANT RULE:* *An object can appear either between or after the two words unless it is a *pronoun*, and then it must appear between the two words.**

Separable phrasal verbs	Inseparable phrasal verbs
put off (postpone)	look for (search)
turn down (reject *or* lower volume)	turn up (appear)
point out (mention, emphasize)	come over (visit)

figure out (understand after thinking)
find out (discover information)
give up (stop trying)

cut out (eliminate)
check out (focus on, to) pay attention
call up (call on the phone)
put on (wear)

run into (meet by accident)

come back (return)
hear from (receive communication from)
take after (be similar to)
cut down (reduce)

get over (recover from)
take place (happen, occur)

More examples with separable phrasal verbs:

Yale turned down **John.** He did not get in.
I also applied, but they turned **me** down, too.
I figured out **the math problem.**

I figured **it** out.
I checked out **the library book.**
I checked **it** out.

All three-word phrasal verbs are inseparable:

run out of (use so that no more is left)
look up to (admire)

look down on (dislike, disapprove)
put up with (tolerate, stand)
get rid of (throw away, discard)
come up with (invent)

PRACTICE 4H: Phrasal Verbs

Choose the best phrasal verb from the ones listed above to fill in the blank.

1. Can you please ______________________ when the baseball game starts?
2. I have not ______________________ Jason in a long time; I'm not even sure where he lives or what he is doing these days.
3. Alexandra ______________________ her mom. They both love to cook and make delicious meals.
4. That is such a great idea! How did you ______________________ that?
5. Sorry, we have ______________________ orange juice. Would you like apple juice instead?

6. I really _______________________ my father. He is the smartest and kindest guy I know.

Circle the best choice of the underlined options.

7. Something surprising happened; I ran into Gary / ran Gary into at the coffee shop.
8. I was a smoker for many years, but I finally gave up it / gave it up last July.
9. Andrew asked Lana out on a date, but she turned him down / turned down him.
10. We lost our cat, and we are looking him for / looking for him all over the neighborhood.

Stative verbs

These verbs are used to describe states of existence or situations that last for a period of time. Many of them relate to the mind, emotional states, using the senses, or possession.

Examples of Common Stative Verbs

The mind:
know, think, understand, believe, recognize, remember, agree, disagree, realize, mean, doubt, suppose, imagine
Emotion:
love, like, dislike, hate, prefer, mind, please, matter, care, satisfy, impress, surprise, shock, wish
The senses:
appear, look, see, seem, taste, sound, hear, smell, perceive
Possession:
own, have, contain, belong, possess, consist, include
Other common stative verbs:
want, need, fit, owe, cost, weigh, depend, deny, promise

IMPORTANT RULE: **These verbs, when used with a stative meaning (a state of existence), are not used with progressive verb forms.**

Incorrect: I am recognizing that girl.

Incorrect: This book is costing six dollars.

Incorrect: Were you owning a car during college?

Some of these verbs have both a stative and nonstative (active/dynamic) meaning. If you use the verbs this way, progressive forms are acceptable:

The pizza tastes good.	=	*taste* as a stative verb, a state of existence.
I'm tasting all the food at the party.	=	*taste* as an active verb, an action.
They have a new car.	=	*have* as a stative verb; it means "own" or "possess."
They are having a party next week.	=	*have* as an active verb; here it means "giving" or "hosting."

TIP

To avoid grammar mistakes, make sure you know if you are using the *stative* or *active* meaning of verbs.

PRACTICE 4I: Stative Verbs

Some of the following sentences have a mistake. Circle the mistakes.

1. This cake is tasting so good. What is the recipe?
2. We were hearing a loud noise, so we went to see what it was.
3. Are you looking at me? Your eyes are hidden by the sunglasses.
4. Charles is owing me fifty dollars.
5. I am having a difficult week, and I can't wait for it to end.

Gerunds and infinitives

- A *gerund* is the *–ing* form of the verb used as a noun: "I like swimming."
- An *infinitive* is *to* + base verb: "I like to swim."

Use the gerund:

1. After certain verbs (as the object):
   "I enjoy dancing."
   Examples: *avoid, recommend, enjoy, discuss, suggest, consider* (Do a web search for "verbs followed by gerunds and infinitives" to consult a word list if you're not sure.)

2. As the subject of a sentence: "Smoking is not allowed." "Dancing is fun."
   (Infinitives can be used this way in writing, but they often sound formal or old-fashioned.)
3. After prepositions:"I thought about studying there."
   Examples: *for, in, of, about, on, up*
4. For recreation ideas after *go*: "I went camping, and then I went shopping."
   Examples: *hiking, running, walking, jogging, sailing, swimming, drinking*

Use the infinitive:

1. After certain verbs: "I decided to travel there."
   Examples: *agree, decide, expect, hope, learn, manage, need, try, want* (Consult a word list if you're not sure.)
2. After *be* + adjective: "We are ready to leave."
   Examples: *happy, willing, ready, prepared*
3. After certain nouns: "She has the ability to fly an airplane."
   Examples: *ability, capacity, need, desire, idea, strength*)
4. For an "in order to" idea: "He read many books to learn about law."

Some verbs can take either a gerund or an infinitive after. Common ones are: *like, love, hate, start, begin, prefer, continue*. Also, some verbs take both, but the meaning changes (e.g., *remember, forget, stop, quit, try, regret*):

I remembered to turn off the lights.	I didn't forget
I remembered turning off the lights.	It was in my memory
I forgot to turn off the lights.	I didn't remember
I forgot turning off the lights.	It wasn't in my memory
I stopped to smoke.	I paused, interrupted another activity
I stopped smoking.	I ceased completely
I quit to work there.	the "in order to" idea
I quit working there.	I ceased completely
I tried to ski.	I attempted it

I tried skiing.	I experienced it for the first time
I regret to say that I am sick.	I'm sorry about right now
I regret saying that I am sick.	I'm sorry about the past

Here are two patterns with *prefer*:

I prefer ________ (gerund) to ____________ (gerund).

I prefer ________ (infinitive) rather than ________ (infinitive).

PRACTICE 4J: Gerund and Infinitive Forms

Add either the gerund or infinitive form of the verb under the blank, depending on which one is correct.

1. I recommend ____________________ (visit) the Statue of Liberty when you're in New York.
2. ________________________ (exercise) is the best way to stay healthy.
3. In that country, they do not have the right _______________ (vote).
4. I remembered _________________________ (call) my mom this weekend. I didn't forget!
5. When I think about high school, I remember the parties, but I don't remember ________________ (study)!
6. I went ________________ (hike) in the Grand Canyon last summer, and I loved it.
7. Are you considering ______________________ (live) in the United States?
8. Did Hal suggest ____________ (go) to a movie or ____________ (go) to a restaurant?

9. I stopped ______________________ after I turned 40
smoke
years old.
10. On my way to the train station, I stopped ______________
buy
some wine.
11. I prefer reading to ______________________.
write
12. You should avoid ______________________ too much
spend
money on your vacation.
13. My brother is not interested in ______________________
come
with us.
14. I tried ______________________ for the first time yesterday, and
skateboard
I really liked it.
15. Carlos came to the United States ______________________
travel
and ______________________ people.
meet

Adjective (relative) clauses

An adjective clause is a clause (a phrase with a **subject** and a **verb**) that gives more information about a noun (and so acts like an adjective):

The **girl** <u>who lives here</u> is really nice
(Tells us more about the girl.)

Where is the **book** <u>that I borrowed from Ross?</u>
(Tells us more about the book.)

Physics, <u>which is considered a complicated subject</u>, is hard to study. (Tells us more about physics.)

1. Adjective clauses usually come right after the noun they modify.
2. In their full form, they have *relative pronouns*:
which for things
who for people
*that** for both things and people

whose for possessive
where for places
when for times
whom for people when they are objects
*Do not use *that* in nonrestrictive clauses.

3. Adjective clauses can be *restrictive* or *nonrestrictive.*
   Restrictive means that the adjective clause is being used to identify the noun:

   "I like the cake that Darcy baked. The other cakes were not so good."

   (Do not place commas around restrictive clauses.)

   Nonrestrictive means that the adjective clause is just giving extra information:

   "The cake, which was baked by Darcy, was delicious. She used a lot of sugar, which made it sweet."

   (Use commas with nonrestrictive clauses.)

4. **Reduced adjective clauses.** Two basic rules:

   A. If the noun being modified in a restrictive adjective clause is the *object* of that clause, then the relative pronoun can be omitted. This is a more casual style, common in speaking:

   "I saw the movie that you mentioned." = "I saw the movie you mentioned."

   "The book that you lent me is here." = "The book you lent me is here."

   "The food, which was not good, did not get eaten." (You **cannot omit** *which* here)

   B. If the adjective clause contains a *be* verb plus *who/which/that*, you can omit *be* and the relative pronoun. Again, this is a more casual style, common in speaking:

   "The girl who is studying over there is Lynn." = "The girl studying over there is Lynn."

   "Many products that are sold here are cheaper." = "Many products sold here are cheaper."

   "The furniture that is in the bedroom is antique." = "The furniture in the bedroom is antique."

C. Appositives

"My father, <u>who</u> <u>is</u> a doctor, knows a lot." = "My father, a doctor, knows a lot."

"Russia, <u>which</u> <u>is</u> the largest country in the world, is huge!" = "Russia, the largest country in the world, is huge!"

When two noun phrases are together like this, referring to the same thing, it is called an *appositive*. Always use a comma between the two noun phrases, to make it clear that you have written an appositive.

PRACTICE 4K: Adjective Clauses

Find and underline the mistakes with adjective clauses in each sentence.

1. One of the people which I respect most is my grandfather.
2. That was the year where I first learned about rock music.
3. Dylan, which parents are coming tonight, needs to clean his dorm room.
4. The students finished the test before noon were allowed to leave.
5. Many things that I've learned in school, they are useful.
6. I don't like most Italian films, but I like the ones, which are directed by Fellini.
7. Harvard an Ivy League university is difficult to get into.
8. The town that I grew up is a very small place.
9. Let me give you the advice which I also gave it to David.
10. There is a bookcase separates the living room from the dining room.

Either, both, neither, so

- *Both* means "the first one *and* the second one."
- *Neither* (in front of a noun or pronoun) means "not the first one and not the second one."
- *Either* (in front of a noun or pronoun) means "one *or* the other of two, but *not* both."

In sentences using *either* and *neither*, where the first and second item are both singular, use a **singular verb form.**

In informal English, you may hear *neither* in these kinds of structures used with a plural verb form, but a singular verb form is the correct written form in academic English.

Use *either* with *or*. Use *neither* with *nor*:

> **Either** the president **or** the prime minister is coming to the meeting. (One or the other is going, but not both.)
>
> "**Neither** Jane **nor** Marty likes the beach."
> (Jane doesn't like the beach. Marty also doesn't like it.)

Only use the word *both* (+ plural verb) when it is an **affirmative** situation about two subjects:

> Both the president and the prime minister **are** coming to the meeting.
>
> Both Jane and Marty **like** the beach.

If there is a negative (*not*) before the verb and the "both" idea is the object, it becomes *either*:

> I don't know either Jane or Marty. I don't know either one.

So versus ***neither*** and ***either*** (meaning "also/also not")

If some subject's situation is also true for the second subject (affirmative), use *so* to mean "also"

So am I.	So has he.	So does Rick.
So can they.	So will Dad.	

If one subject's situation is also true for a second subject—but **negative**—use *neither* to mean "also":

Neither am I.	Neither does Rick.	Neither has he.
Neither will Dad.	Neither can they.	

The *so* or *neither* goes before the helping (auxiliary) verb; the subject goes after.

> ***Reminder:*** **Auxiliary (helping) verbs** in English are *be*, *do*, *have*, and the modal verbs.

If the "also" idea is at the **end of a sentence** with a negative structure, *either* is used:

> We didn't go either. I didn't like it either.
> Diana doesn't speak Italian either.

PRACTICE 4L: Either, Both, Neither, So

Circle the best choice from the underlined choices.

1. Both / Either / Neither teachers were feeling sick, so there was no one to teach the class.
2. I was offered two desserts, but I didn't like both / either / neither of them.
3. Both / Either / Neither Jack nor Luke came to English class today.
4. You can get to Brown Hall both / either / neither by walking around the library or going through the gym.
5. I talked to both / either / neither of them and told them what had happened.
6. I went home to see my parents, but neither was / were there.
7. Venezuela exports a lot of oil, and so does / so is / neither does / neither is Saudi Arabia.
8. Maxim is living here now, but he's originally from Russia, and so I am / so am I / so I did / so did I.
9. Chang did not answer every question on the test, and I didn't neither / either / so / both.
10. The movie was not as good as the original book, and so was / so were / neither was / neither were the play.

Conditional sentences

Conditional sentences are sentences with an "if" idea. They usually have an "if" clause and a "result" clause:

> If it rains tomorrow, I will bring an umbrella.
> "if" clause — "result" clause

The order or sequence of these clauses can be either *if* + result, **or** result + *if*:

> I will bring an umbrella if it rains tomorrow.

Remember: use a comma after the "if" clause when it goes first, since it is a dependent clause.

Present/future conditions usually have the same essential grammar. The **past** works differently.

Here are the basic and most commonly used conditional sentence types:

1. **Real (present/future): simple present** in "if" clause | **simple present** or **future** (or modal) in "result" clause. This structure can be about results now or in the future.

   If it is about a result **now**, the word *if* can be substituted by the word *when*:

   If you heat water, it boils. = When you heat water, it boils.

   If I'm done with homework, I watch TV at night. = When I'm done with homework, I watch TV at night.

   Future real conditionals have results that are not certain:

   If it is too cold tomorrow, we will cancel the picnic.

   We are going to see Sandra if she comes to California.

   They might visit us if they have enough time.

2. **Unreal (present/future): past simple** in "if" clause | *would/could/might* + base verb in "result" clause.

   Be is always in *were* form in these sentence types:

   If I had enough time, I would watch TV. [But I don't.]

   If we had a car, we could drive to the city. [But we don't.]

   Dave might eat more vegetables if he knew about nutrition. [But he doesn't.]

   A more formal-sounding structure, found mostly in writing, is ***if* + *were* + infinitive:**

   If we were to realize the truth, we might be very surprised.

3. **Past unreal: past perfect** in "if" clause | *would/could/might* + *have* + past participle in "result" clause:

   If I had arrived there on time, I might have seen Joe (but I didn't).

   If she had known about the lecture, she probably would have gone.

We could have eaten something at the hotel if we had not been so rushed!

They would have called sooner if they had understood how urgent it was.

Note that there is no "past real" conditional form.

Other kinds of conditional sentences:

4. **Mixed conditionals**

   These are less common. The tense of the "if" clause and the tense of the result clause are different:

   If the kitchen is dirty [now], then Dave forgot to clean it [last night].

   Marie will not do well on the test [tomorrow] if she ignored the homework [during the past semester].

   If I had studied harder [in the past], I would not be worried about my grades [now].

5. ***If* replacements**

   The modal *should* can be used in the "if" clause instead of the word *if*. It goes in front of the subject (this is a formal-sounding form):

   If Carla arrives early, we'll walk there. → Should Carla arrive early, we'll walk there.

   If can be **omitted before past perfect verbs,** but then, *had* moves in front of the subject:

   If I had known, I would have said something. → Had I known, I would have said something.

   If can be replaced with ***only if, provided that,*** or ***as long as*** for a very strict/limited condition:

   I will lend you the money you need **only if / as long as / provided that** you pay me back quickly.

   Unless is a kind of "if" clause. It means "except if":

   We will have lunch outside tomorrow unless it rains.

   Unless you're busy, I'd like to invite you to dinner.

In case or ***in the event that*** also mean *if*:

I will bring extra clothes **in case / in the event that** I stay overnight."

"Wish" statements are similar to unreal conditional sentences.

There are five common structures used with the verb *wish*:

Present:

1. *wish* + ***would/could*** (+ base verb):
   I wish I could fly. She wishes he would go away.
2. *wish* + **past tense:**
   I wish I spoke Spanish. You wish I did also!
3. *wish* + ***were*** (for "be" wishes):
   I wish I were rich. They wish she were coming tomorrow.

Past:

4. *wish* + ***had*** + **past participle:**
   I wish I had known that! I wish you had seen it.
5. *wish* + ***could have*** + **past participle:**
   I wish I could have slept. She wishes I could have gone.

Do not use *would* in the past tense in these "wish" statements. The verb *hope* is common for the idea of a wish for the future.

TIP
Avoid confusion between *wish* (an *unreal* idea) and *hope* (a possible, and therefore real idea).

PRACTICE 4M: Conditional and "Wish" Sentences

Identify and try to correct the mistakes used with these conditional and "wish" sentences.

1. Should you will need me, I will be in the library.
2. We will try to see Monica in Paris this summer if we had enough time.
3. We could speak Hindi with Nisha if we know how to, but we don't.
4. If Diana knew about the planning meeting yesterday, she would probably go.

5. We could gone to the tennis match, but we decided not to.
6. Had I written this essay more carefully, there weren't so many errors.
7. I can't get a certificate for this course unless I would attend every class.
8. Sam wishes he was thinner; then he could wear this suit.
9. I wish I would have taken an art history class in college.
10. Do you ever wish you know a celebrity?

Articles

Articles operate like adjectives. They are used to identify or give information about nouns. Using articles correctly can be tricky for some nonnative users of English because articles are used so differently in different languages. Some languages have no articles (e.g., Chinese and Russian), and some have many (German has twelve!).

English has two **indefinite articles:**

a (before words that start with a consonant sound) "I see **a** mountain." ↑consonant sound

an (before words that start with a vowel sound) "I see **an** enormous mountain." ↑vowel sound

English has one **definite article:**

the "I see **the** mountain that we climbed yesterday."
definite thing, defined specifically

In many cases, no article (**zero article,** represented by this: Ø) is appropriate before a noun. This is often true for uncountable nouns and plural nouns:

"When it comes to ^ fruit, I would rather eat ^ apples than ^ bananas."
(fruit: ~~the~~ ~~an~~; apples: ~~the~~ ~~an~~; bananas: ~~the~~ ~~a~~)

Although there are rules about using articles in English, the rules can be a bit complicated and not fail-safe. In fact, some language teachers will say that the only way to really learn to use articles in a natural, error-free way is to read a lot of English and "absorb" how they are used in the language for yourself. To some extent, this is true. For example, there are many fixed expressions that use articles in a specific way (e.g., "all in *a* day's work"), which might not be familiar to English language learners. An attempt to list *all* of the rules and uses of articles in English might constitute its own book! In any case, here are some of the basic rules you can apply to avoid mistakes with articles:

1. An indefinite article is used to classify a type of noun, not a specific example:

a mountain	an elephant	a mystery novel
an area of science	a type of fruit	

   These kinds of nouns are sometimes called *generic* nouns.

2. A definite article is used to identify a specific noun:

the mountain that we climbed	the elephant at the zoo
the book on the table	

   These kinds of nouns are sometimes called *concrete* nouns.

3. You cannot use *a* or *an* before plural nouns or uncountable nouns, including gerunds. (See page 64 for a review of uncountable nouns.)

4. The definite article is used with unique noun phrases (e.g., *the* earth; *the* only solution), superlative forms (e.g., *the* best choice), before ordinal numbers (e.g., *the* second day), before specific parts of a group (e.g., *the* second half; *the* north side), and before nouns that are followed by an "of" phrase (e.g., *the* disadvantages of his plan; *the* results of research).

5. The rules for using articles with geographical terms are quite specific:

   Do *not* use any article for these:

   Continents: Africa, Europe, Asia, Antarctica, Australia, South America, North America, etc.

   City names and their districts: Paris, Tokyo, Riyadh, New York, etc. (There are some exceptions, such as the Hague, the Bronx.)

   Park names: Central Park, MacArthur Park, etc.

   Most country (political division) names: Germany, Korea, Egypt, Argentina, etc. There are, however, exceptions in which the word *the* is used. For example: the United States, the United Kingdom, the Philippines, the Netherlands, and any country with "Republic" in its name (e.g., the Czech Republic, the Dominican Republic).

TIP

When you write the name of the United States in any form, except as an adjective such as "U.S. citizen" or "U.S. dollars," don't forget to use *the* (*the* United States, *the* United States of America, *the* USA). Otherwise, you are making a grammar mistake!

Always use *the* with proper names of rivers, seas, oceans, gulfs, and deserts:

the Hudson River
the Baltic Sea
the Indian Ocean
the Persian Gulf
the Sahara Desert

Following are sets of related noun categories in which some types need *the* and some do not:

Individual mountains (no *the*) Mount Fuji, Mt. Everest	**Mountain ranges (use *the*)** the Rocky Mountains, the Alps
Islands Easter Island, Manhattan, Maui	**Groups of islands** the West Indies, the Bahamas
Lakes Lake Ontario, Lake Como	**Groups of lakes** the Great Lakes, the East African Lakes
Directions (without prepositions) right, left, west, southeast	**Directions (after prepositions)** to the right, in the Southwest, across the Northeast

Practice 4N: Articles

Correctly add either *the*, *a*, *an*, or Ø in the space provided.

1. This is _____ only policy _____ president supports for trade with Canada.
2. He asked me for _____ dollar, but I don't have one to lend him.
3. _____ swimming pool is _____ most unique feature of this hotel.

4. Did you hear _____ news about Juan? He is moving back to _____Los Angeles!
5. I have _____ idea that I would like to share with you.
6. There is _____ basement underneath _____ building where I live.
7. _____ Americans do not value _____ cooking as much as French people do.
8. The refugees moved from _____ Uganda to _____Democratic Republic of the Congo.
9. _____ High Park is _____ largest park in _____ Toronto.
10. _____ name of _____ movie we saw last night is *Over _____ Atlantic.*

Idioms and Collocations

Idioms

Idioms are phrases that have a *figurative* (rather than literal) meaning. As an example, if you say "I have a pain in my neck," and rub your neck with your hand while moving your head around, a listener will understand that you mean a literal pain in your neck. On the other hand, if you say, "My brother is a pain in the neck!" a listener will understand that you are using the idiom "pain in the neck," which means "annoying," and you are not literally talking about a pain, or about your neck. Not all idioms make sense literally. For example, "quit cold turkey" means to stop a habit immediately rather than gradually. If someone tells you that they quit smoking cigarettes "cold turkey," you might be able to guess that this is an idiom, even though you don't know it because it makes no sense literally. It is not about coldness or turkey. Because idioms are figurative language, they are similar to phrasal verbs. You often cannot guess the meaning, and you need to learn them as new vocabulary. (For a review of phrasal verbs, see page 79.)

There are two issues connected with idioms that you should keep in mind:

1. Try to learn and remember as many idioms as you can, for comprehension. Learn to recognize idioms in spoken and written English. Knowledge of idioms is essential for communicating effectively. If you encounter a new idiom and are not sure

about its meaning, ask someone or look it up in a book or online. One recommended book for self-study on idioms is *Essential Idioms in English* by Robert J. Dixson (Pearson Longman). A useful Internet resource is FreeDictionary.com at idioms.thefreedictionary.com/.

2. If you can use English idioms naturally and effectively, it will make your writing more fluent and sophisticated. Certain idioms, such as "on the other hand," are very common in academic writing and are *set phrases*, meaning you have to use those words, all of those words, and only those words to convey the meaning you intend. It is important to keep in mind, however, that some idioms—for example, "What's up?"—are too informal or too much like slang to be appropriate for academic writing. If you're not sure, ask your instructor or a native speaker. Also, some idioms are so overused that they will make your writing sound unoriginal; such idioms are often referred to by the French word *cliché*. Your instructor may suggest that you reword something you have written to avoid using a cliché.

Sample list of some common idioms found in academic English:

Idiom	Meaning
Nouns	
the bottom line	the main idea/most important idea
the big picture	the complete view of a situation
a litmus test	an indicator of future success or failure
a rule of thumb	a guideline
Adjectives	
more or less	somewhat; sort of
out of the question	impossible; definitely not
Verbs	
on the same page	to have the same understanding about a subject
come into play	to be a participant or a factor in some thing
get a handle on (a situation)	to gain understanding of a situation

get to the bottom of it	figure out what really happened in a situation
go off on a tangent	change the subject to something irrelevant
go hand-in-hand with (something)	be very closely linked with something
it goes to show	it proves
shift gears	to change the subject
split hairs	to make trivial distinctions
take (something) for granted	to assume to be true
ring a bell	to sound familiar
Prepositional phrases	
by far	this is very much the case
in a nutshell	in summary

Collocations

Collocations are word pairs that occur very frequently together in English. There are no rules for what makes a collocation; they're just words that English speakers put together out of convention. If you notice the same word combination two or three times, it could be a common collocation. These word combinations have become a common way to express certain ideas in English. Unlike idioms, which are always figurative, collocations usually use words in their literal meaning, so they are easier to comprehend.

As with idioms, your English will sound more natural if you use collocations in your speech and writing. Collocations can be different parts of speech; for example, *inextricably linked* is a common adjective–noun collocation that literally means "so closely connected that you cannot separate them." You could write something like: "nutritious food and good health are closely connected," or that they are "strongly related," and you are conveying the same idea, but if you use the collocation *inextricably linked,* your language sounds more like well-written academic English.

Dire consequences is an example of a common **adjective–noun collocation**. It means "negative results." *Apologize profusely* is an example of a common **verb–adverb collocation**. It means "greatly apologize." There are many collocation dictionaries you can use. A helpful free online resource is the *Oxford Online Collocations Dictionary* at www.lixiaolai.com/ocd/.

Sample list of common collocations found in academic English:

Collocation	Meaning
extenuating circumstances	factors that should be considered in decision making
an exorbitant cost	a very high cost, perhaps too high
utter nonsense	complete nonsense; completely untrue
widespread support	a lot of support; approved of by many people
a far-fetched theory	a theory that is not likely or feasible
a full-scale investigation	a thorough investigation of a situation
an ill-conceived plan	poorly thought-out idea
the worst-case scenario	the worst possible future outcome
to wreak havoc	to cause destruction
to elicit a reaction	to cause a certain response
to file a lawsuit	to bring a lawsuit in court

Useful websites

The following websites are very useful for students who are learning English.

Dictionary	Longman Dictionary of Contemporary English www.ldoceonline.com/
Idioms	The FreeDictionary.com idioms.thefreedictionary.com/
Collocations	Oxford Collocations Dictionary online www.lixiaolai.com/ocd/
Writing help	Purdue University Online Writing Lab owl.english.purdue.edu/
Grammar Guides	Capital Community College grammar.ccc.commnet.edu/grammar/
Listening Comprehension	
Practice (news)	VOA Special English News for English Learners www.voanews.com/learningenglish/home/
Practice (lectures)	TED.com, www.ted.com

Appendix

Answer Key to Exercises in Chapter 4

PRACTICE 4A

1. verb
2. noun
3. adj.
4. verb (past)
5. adj.
6. adj.
7. noun
8. verb
9. noun
10. adj.
11. noun
12. adj.
13. verb
14. adv
15. noun (person)
16. noun (idea)
17. adj.
18. noun (thing)
19. adj.
20. adv.
21. noun
22. verb
23. noun
24. adj.
25. adv.
26. adj.
27. verb
28. creativity (noun)
29. beautify (verb)
30. successful (adj.)
31. opposed (adj.)
32. economy (noun)
33. controversial (adj.)
34. improve (verb)
35. connected (adj.)

PRACTICE 4B

1. vocabulary; slang
2. too much homework
3. too many dollars
4. How many times; we don't have enough time
5. energy
6. advice
7. equipment; furniture
8. at least 50 pieces of clothing
9. information; research
10. snow; rain; that weather

PRACTICE 4C

1. It is so cold here in the winter.
2. It is so fun to go to Disney World.
3. ...it is going to be a really fun party.
4. ...it is almost 2:00!
5. ...it is difficult to hear...

PRACTICE 4D

1. I (must *or* have to: choose one) go to English class now.
2. If you go to China, you (must *or* have to) get a visa beforehand.
3. It (could/might/may/will) rain tomorrow.
4. When you swim underwater, you (must *or* have to) come up to breath air.
5. Jonathan (could/may/might) be in the bathroom right now. I'm not sure.
6. I (had to) go to see my dentist yesterday, so I missed the class.
7. Erin (had to) pick her kids up from school, so she couldn't come to the concert.
8. You should not (have taken) the money which did not belong to you.
9. I saw the movie today; Paul (could/may/might have seen) it yesterday.
10. Marcy (used to) drink coffee every morning, but she stopped.

PRACTICE 4E

1. swam
2. she is
3. played
4. saw
5. thought it was

PRACTICE 4F

1. Have you ever taken
2. we have decided
3. walked
4. died
5. have you visited

PRACTICE 4G

1. I will
2. we're going to
3. departs
4. get
5. is

PRACTICE 4H

1. find out
2. heard from
3. takes after
4. come up with
5. run out of
6. look up to
7. I ran into Gary
8. gave it up
9. turned him down
10. looking for him

PRACTICE 4I

1. This cake is tastes so good...
2. We heard a loud noise...
3. Sentence is correct.
4. Charles owes me fifty dollars.
5. Sentence is correct.

PRACTICE 4J

1. visiting
2. Exercising
3. to vote
4. to call
5. studying
6. hiking
7. living
8. going, going
9. smoking
10. to buy
11. writing
12. spending
13. coming
14. skateboarding
15. to travel, to meet

PRACTICE 4K

1. whom I respect...
2. when I first learned about rock music
3. whose parents are coming
4. The students who *or* that finished the test before noon were allowed to leave.
5. Many things that I've learned in school are useful (no *they*)
6. ... I like the ones which are directed by Fellini (no comma)
7. Harvard, an Ivy League university, is difficult to get into (add commas)
8. The town where I grew up...
9. ...which I also gave to David (no *it*)
10. There is a bookcase which *or* that separates the living room from the dining room.

PRACTICE 4L

1. Both
2. either
3. Neither
4. either
5. both
6. was
7. so does
8. so am I
9. either
10. neither was

PRACTICE 4M

1. Should you need me…
2. …if we have enough time
3. …if we knew how to…
4. If Diana had known…she would probably have gone *or* probably would have gone
5. We could have gone to the tennis match…
6. …there would not be (now) or would not have been so many errors.
7. …unless I attend every class.
8. Sam wishes he were thinner…
9. I wish I had taken an art history class in college.
10. Do you ever wish you knew a celebrity?

PRACTICE 4N

1. the, the
2. a
3. the, the
4. the, Ø
5. an
6. a, the
7. Ø, Ø
8. Ø, the
9. Ø, the, Ø
10. the, the, the